# Service Learning Projects for Elementary Students

## by Deborah Diffily
## and Charlotte Sassman

**Carson-Dellosa Publishing**
**Greensboro, North Carolina**

## Credits

**Project Director**
Jennifer Weaver-Spencer

**Layout Design**
Jon Nawrocik

**Inside Illustrations**
Wayne Miller

**Cover Design**
Peggy Jackson

ISBN 1-59441-058-5

# Contents

## What Are Service Projects?

Why Do Service Projects? . . . . . . . . . . . . . . . . . . . . . . 5
Not Just for Older Students . . . . . . . . . . . . . . . . . . . . 6
Learning During Service Project Work . . . . . . . . . . 6
Benefits of Service Learning to Students . . . . . . . . . 6
   Establishing a Community through Service
   Projects . . . . . . . . . . . . . . . . . . . . . . . . . . . . . . . . 7
   Expanding Students' Empathy for Others . . . . . . 7
   Developing Competent and Capable People . . . . 8
   Developing Leadership Qualities at an Early Age  8
Benefits for the Community in General . . . . . . . . . . 8
Possible Service Projects . . . . . . . . . . . . . . . . . . . . . 8
   Doing Personal Service Projects . . . . . . . . . . . . . 8
   Responding to Needs within the School . . . . . . . 9
   Responding to Local Needs . . . . . . . . . . . . . . . . 9
   Supporting Local Organizations . . . . . . . . . . . . 9
Summary . . . . . . . . . . . . . . . . . . . . . . . . . . . . . . . . . . 9

## The Story of One Service Project: A Canned Food Drive

The Canned Food Collection . . . . . . . . . . . . . . . . . 10
   Announcing the Need . . . . . . . . . . . . . . . . . . . . 10
   Responding to the Need . . . . . . . . . . . . . . . . . . 10
   Planning the Work . . . . . . . . . . . . . . . . . . . . . . 11
   Expanding the Focus . . . . . . . . . . . . . . . . . . . . 12
   Sharing the Work . . . . . . . . . . . . . . . . . . . . . . . 12
   Interviewing the "Experts" . . . . . . . . . . . . . . . . 12
   Beginning the Drive . . . . . . . . . . . . . . . . . . . . . 13
   Collecting the Food . . . . . . . . . . . . . . . . . . . . . 13
   Proceeding Day-to-Day . . . . . . . . . . . . . . . . . . 14
   Making Observations about the Collection . . . . 14
   Solving the Problem . . . . . . . . . . . . . . . . . . . . . 14
   Ending the Drive . . . . . . . . . . . . . . . . . . . . . . . 15
Summary . . . . . . . . . . . . . . . . . . . . . . . . . . . . . . . . . 15
Knowledge and Skills Embedded in the Canned Food
Drive Project . . . . . . . . . . . . . . . . . . . . . . . . . . . . . . 16

## Characteristics of Projects

Student Directed . . . . . . . . . . . . . . . . . . . . . . . . . . 19
Research Based . . . . . . . . . . . . . . . . . . . . . . . . . . . 21
Multiple Resources Consulted . . . . . . . . . . . . . . . . 22
Connected to the Real World . . . . . . . . . . . . . . . . . 22
Embedded with Knowledge and Skills . . . . . . . . . 23
Summary . . . . . . . . . . . . . . . . . . . . . . . . . . . . . . . . . 23

## The Project-Based Classroom

Meeting Areas . . . . . . . . . . . . . . . . . . . . . . . . . . . . 24
Classroom Arrangement . . . . . . . . . . . . . . . . . . . . 26
Supplies . . . . . . . . . . . . . . . . . . . . . . . . . . . . . . . . . 26
Resources . . . . . . . . . . . . . . . . . . . . . . . . . . . . . . . . 27
Student Work . . . . . . . . . . . . . . . . . . . . . . . . . . . . . 28
Summary . . . . . . . . . . . . . . . . . . . . . . . . . . . . . . . . . 29

## The Project-Based Community

Getting to Know Each Other . . . . . . . . . . . . . . . . . 30
Developing a Caring Atmosphere . . . . . . . . . . . . . 31
Establishing Routines . . . . . . . . . . . . . . . . . . . . . . 32
Learning to Make Decisions . . . . . . . . . . . . . . . . . 33
Voting . . . . . . . . . . . . . . . . . . . . . . . . . . . . . . . . . . 34
Reaching Consensus . . . . . . . . . . . . . . . . . . . . . . . 34
Leading but Not Telling . . . . . . . . . . . . . . . . . . . . 35
Accepting Responsibility . . . . . . . . . . . . . . . . . . . . 36
Learning to Communicate . . . . . . . . . . . . . . . . . . . 36
Learning to Solve Problems . . . . . . . . . . . . . . . . . . 37
Conflict Resolution . . . . . . . . . . . . . . . . . . . . . . . . 37
Solving Work-Related Problems . . . . . . . . . . . . . . 38
Summary . . . . . . . . . . . . . . . . . . . . . . . . . . . . . . . . . 38

## The Academic Learning Embedded in Projects

Reading . . . . . . . . . . . . . . . . . . . . . . . . . . . . . . . . . 39
Writing . . . . . . . . . . . . . . . . . . . . . . . . . . . . . . . . . 40

# Contents (cont.)

Math . . . . . . . . . . . . . . . . . . . . . . . . . . . . . . . . . 42
Social Studies . . . . . . . . . . . . . . . . . . . . . . . . . . 43
Science . . . . . . . . . . . . . . . . . . . . . . . . . . . . . . . 44
Thinking and Reasoning Skills . . . . . . . . . . . . . 44
Learning How to Learn . . . . . . . . . . . . . . . . . . 45
Summary . . . . . . . . . . . . . . . . . . . . . . . . . . . . . 45

## Social and Emotional Development in Service Projects

Enhancing Children's Social-Emotional
    Development . . . . . . . . . . . . . . . . . . . . . . . . . 46
    Interactions with Others . . . . . . . . . . . . . . . . 46
    Individual Qualities . . . . . . . . . . . . . . . . . . . 47
    Fostering Personal Skills . . . . . . . . . . . . . . . . 48
    Establishing Good Citizens for the Future . . . . 50
Summary . . . . . . . . . . . . . . . . . . . . . . . . . . . . . 50

## The Steps in a Service Project

Before the Project . . . . . . . . . . . . . . . . . . . . . . 51
Introducing the Project to Students . . . . . . . . . . 52
Initial Planning . . . . . . . . . . . . . . . . . . . . . . . . 52
Creating Committees . . . . . . . . . . . . . . . . . . . . 52
Creating Due Dates . . . . . . . . . . . . . . . . . . . . . 53
Holding Planning and Check-In Meetings . . . . . . 53
Tracking Progress . . . . . . . . . . . . . . . . . . . . . . 54
Wrapping Up the Project . . . . . . . . . . . . . . . . . 54
Assessing the Finished Project . . . . . . . . . . . . . . 55
Evaluation of Project . . . . . . . . . . . . . . . . . . . . 55
Summary . . . . . . . . . . . . . . . . . . . . . . . . . . . . . 56

## Identifying School and Community Needs

School-Based Needs . . . . . . . . . . . . . . . . . . . . . 57
Service Projects That Benefit Teachers . . . . . . . . 58
Service Projects That Benefit Students . . . . . . . . 59
Service Projects That Benefit the Entire School
    Community . . . . . . . . . . . . . . . . . . . . . . . . . 60
Community-Based Needs . . . . . . . . . . . . . . . . . 63
Summary . . . . . . . . . . . . . . . . . . . . . . . . . . . . . 64

## Appendix

Coupons for All Project . . . . . . . . . . . . . . . . . . 65
Mittens and Gloves Tree Project . . . . . . . . . . . . 66
School Lost and Found Project . . . . . . . . . . . . . 67
PTA Membership Drive Project . . . . . . . . . . . . . 68
Book Drive Project . . . . . . . . . . . . . . . . . . . . . 69
Reading Service Project . . . . . . . . . . . . . . . . . . 71
Other Ideas for K-5 Service Projects . . . . . . . . . 73
References . . . . . . . . . . . . . . . . . . . . . . . . . . . . 74

## Reproducibles

Ideas for Service Projects . . . . . . . . . . . . . . . . . 75
Phone Call Planning Sheet . . . . . . . . . . . . . . . . . 76
Form for Writing Announcements . . . . . . . . . . . 77
Advertising Planning Sheet . . . . . . . . . . . . . . . . 78
Committee Task Sheet . . . . . . . . . . . . . . . . . . . 79
Bar Graph . . . . . . . . . . . . . . . . . . . . . . . . . . . . 80
Thermometer Graph . . . . . . . . . . . . . . . . . . . . . 81
Characteristics of Projects . . . . . . . . . . . . . . . . 82
Academic Learning Checklist . . . . . . . . . . . . . . 83
Supplies List . . . . . . . . . . . . . . . . . . . . . . . . . . 84
Request for Resources Form . . . . . . . . . . . . . . . 85
Personal Poem . . . . . . . . . . . . . . . . . . . . . . . . . 86
Personal Interest Bingo . . . . . . . . . . . . . . . . . . 87
Thanks Cards . . . . . . . . . . . . . . . . . . . . . . . . . 88
Respectful Classroom Language . . . . . . . . . . . . . 89
Self-Assessment I . . . . . . . . . . . . . . . . . . . . . . . 90
Self-Assessment II . . . . . . . . . . . . . . . . . . . . . . 91
Blank Calendar . . . . . . . . . . . . . . . . . . . . . . . . 92
To-Do List . . . . . . . . . . . . . . . . . . . . . . . . . . . 93
Grid for Classroom Arrangement . . . . . . . . . . . . 94
Voting Chart . . . . . . . . . . . . . . . . . . . . . . . . . . 95
Notes . . . . . . . . . . . . . . . . . . . . . . . . . . . . . . . 96

# What Are Service Projects?

Service projects combine the research-based academic learning of project-based learning with the social/emotional and personal development associated with volunteerism. More and more elementary school teachers are incorporating service projects into their curriculums because these teachers recognize the powerful learning environment that projects provide and the personal changes that take place in their students as they work on service projects.

Schools have long supported outreach activities, or "doing good deeds," such as soliciting donations of gently-used clothing or collecting money for worthy causes. Students have sponsored an acre to preserve a rain forest, adopted an animal from the local zoo, and donated food for hungry people. Traditionally, service activities like this have been initiated by adults, and the learning involved in "doing the good deed" has been fairly limited. The service projects discussed in this book involve students at a much deeper level and enhance both students' academic learning and social development.

During the course of a project, students apply academic and social skills to their project-related work. The organizations that benefit from service projects may be the same ones associated with the service activities completed in the past, but in service projects, the students' involvement is much stronger and their learning is expanded—children lead the decision making and complete the work. Service projects facilitate the application of academic learning to social situations and real-life experiences. Thus, each project becomes a vehicle for learning, not just a "good deed" children are doing.

## Note to the Reader

*Begin to think about projects that your school does to help those who are less fortunate. This notion of "less fortunate" can range from another class in the school who "does not know as much as your class" to homeless children who need clothing. List these projects and think about ways the service activities you are already doing could be extended to become service projects.*

## Why Do Service Projects?

Elementary educators want their students to learn the academic content mandated by their states or provinces and school districts. They want to enhance students' abilities to read and comprehend different genres. They want students to learn how to write conventionally and more effectively. They want students to use mathematical skills to solve real problems. And, they want students to use social studies and science strategies to extend their own learning.

But, teachers also want more for their students. They want each student to develop a sense of responsibility, confidence, initiative, perseverance, and common sense. They want students to learn how to interact with peers in respectful ways and learn how to work as team members. They want students to learn to make good decisions and to solve problems. In short, teachers want students to become good people who will become successful adults. Many attitudes and personal characteristics that contribute to successful adult lives are established in the first decade of a child's life. So, the experiences children have in elementary school dramatically affect the attitudes and personal characteristics that they develop. Many elementary school teachers have discovered that they can teach content <u>and</u> character through service projects.

## Not Just for Older Students

Most people are familiar with service learning in schools, but the vast majority of service learning involves older students. Many high schools and universities have ongoing programs in which students volunteer to work in community service organizations. However, the majority of these programs focus on volunteerism. Students are matched to community organizations, and what students learn tends to be random, based solely on the experiences they have within the organizations.

Elementary educators have examined adolescent service learning and concluded that the learning associated with service learning can be much more purposeful. When service learning is organized into project-based learning, these experiences offer rich learning experiences, as well as other benefits, to elementary-aged students. Children as young as kindergartners benefit from working on service projects. In addition to internalizing the importance of volunteerism, young children can gain important knowledge and skills.

## Learning During Service Project Work

While students are involved in service projects, their learning can be multifaceted. Properly organized service projects offer rich academic learning experiences for students. Students can learn important knowledge and skills mandated by government and district standards. Most service projects require a certain amount of expository reading. Teachers use newspaper and magazine articles, brochures, pamphlets, and Internet sites to teach various reading strategies. A wide variety of writing forms is used during service projects, and teachers incorporate many writing concepts and skills into the writing children do for projects. Numerous math skills are needed as children plan and implement projects. Teachers identify these skills before beginning projects and use math time to teach these skills.

Because children learn the knowledge and skills the teacher targets for each project within the context of doing work that they consider important, they learn more quickly and remember what they learn for longer periods of time. Service projects impact elementary-aged children's cognitive, social, and affective development, often in ways that do not become evident until years later.

## Benefits of Service Learning to Students

Articles about service learning (Brotherton, 2002; Clark, 2002; Gehring, 2002; Jennings, 2001; Johnson, 2001; Waldstein & Reiher, 2001) document the benefits that students receive from working on service learning projects. Students learn important skills related to working with groups. They learn to negotiate and compromise. They learn to use certain people's strengths to accomplish tasks. They learn to plan projects and implement those plans. They learn to make decisions and solve problems. As students work on service projects, they literally learn the skills to get things done. When students work on service projects, they are introduced to topics that they might not otherwise encounter.

For example, when Janet was a third-grade student, she was involved in a service project focused on the celebration of the school's 75th anniversary. The third graders gathered artifacts and school memorabilia and confirmed facts about the school's history. They interviewed alumni and used the information to write a narrative of the school's history. The project culminated with a reunion of more than 300 former students. Now, as a tenth grader, Janet is deeply involved in researching the genealogy of her family and connecting it to occurrences in the world during those times. Janet says, "I just got interested in history when I was in the third grade when we did that project about the school's history. When I'm in college, I think I want to major in American history and focus on oral history." While all students will not discover their college majors or life work during elementary school service projects, working on projects that benefit other people nonetheless provides rich learning experiences.

The level of involvement required of students working on service projects promotes an increased awareness of what it means to contribute to society. Most students, and even many adults, do not realize the role that volunteerism and other forms of philanthropy play in communities. Active involvement in service projects helps students understand how individuals and organizations depend on people's generosity to meet their needs.

## Establishing a Community through Service Projects

Working on service projects extends the sense of community that students feel about their classes and their schools. Students who attend schools where a sense of community is built by caring adults learn to care about each other and are willing to help each other in various ways. When students work on service projects, their sense of community expands beyond the "school family" to include people in their neighborhoods and city. Over time, students view themselves as part of the community as a whole. They begin to feel a sense of community with many different groups of people. From this more global sense of community, students become willing to help people whom they have never met, simply because these people are part of the community and need help.

## Expanding Students' Empathy for Others

Service projects often take students into parts of their community they might not otherwise go. When students venture into different parts of their community, their world views expand. Children subconsciously assume that the rest of the world is similar to what they see in their own lives. As they discover that this is not necessarily true, students' appreciation of diversity is enhanced.

Being part of a group that meets the needs of other people instills in students a true sense of accomplishment and pride. When they work on service learning projects, students accomplish important tasks. Feeling a sense of accomplishment is a natural response to helping meet the needs of others. And, because children work as a group on service projects, <u>all</u> students experience a sense of pride.

## Developing Competent and Capable People

Students of all ages benefit from involvement in service projects. Working on service projects helps establish important values in young children. When they choose projects and direct their work, students are empowered. Many young children do not view themselves as capable of helping others. When they see that they can make important contributions, they see themselves as capable and competent people. This project experience is often the first time students make contributions to other people's lives or to society as a whole.

Young children are naturally egocentric. Developmentally, they see themselves as the centers of the world. It takes time and experiences to support children's abilities to empathize and sympathize with other people. Service learning supports this development.

## Developing Leadership Qualities at an Early Age

Finally, working on service projects builds leaders, especially in students who already demonstrate a strength in what Gardner (1983) labeled the interpersonal intelligence. Hatch (1990) proposed four components of interpersonal intelligence: organizing groups; negotiating solutions; personal connection by using the ability to recognize and respond appropriately to other people's feelings; and social connection with other people, even strangers. These abilities are used throughout the course of service projects and can be enhanced with repeated use.

# Benefits for the Community in General

Many cultural, educational, and social service organizations could not function without the financial support and people resources provided by board members and other volunteers. Museums, symphonies, dance companies, theater groups, and informal education enrichment classes thrive in communities where citizens support them through monetary donations or volunteer efforts. Social service programs that support families in need operate on funds provided by generous corporations, foundations, and individuals. As children work on service projects related to social service programs, they begin to understand that it takes many people willing to give their money and time to sustain the nonprofit organizations in their communities.

# Possible Service Projects

There are many service projects appropriate for elementary-aged students. These fall into four primary categories: providing personal service, responding to specific needs within their school, responding to specific needs in their community, and supporting the work of local organizations. Each type of service learning project can be limited or expansive. It is almost always better to begin with smaller, more limited projects as children and teachers begin to learn how to implement projects.

## Doing Personal Service Projects

Personal service projects, as their name implies, provide services to particular people—other students, teachers, students' families, or community members. These projects can be as simple as a class of older elementary students who read to younger students, or something as large as students organizing a beginning-of-the-year school supply service for families of the school's students. Reaching beyond serving other people in the school, personal service projects might involve keeping a local park clean, or "adopting" senior citizens who live at local nursing facilities.

## Responding to Needs within the School

Many service projects respond to needs within the school. These projects could include organizing the school's lost and found, spearheading the membership drive for the Parent-Teacher Association, or beautifying a portion of the school grounds. Older students can make audiotapes of popular children's books to add to the kindergarten and first-grade listening centers. Students of any grade level (after a certain amount of training) can serve as conflict mediators for their peers. Students can organize many events that adults in traditional elementary schools organize, such as carnivals, talent shows, and kindergarten orientation.

## Responding to Local Needs

**Note to the Reader**

*Go back to the list you started at the beginning of this chapter. Determine whether the things you listed can be organized into the four categories discussed in this chapter. See page 75 for a reproducible to help you organize your ideas for projects. Rearrange your list and think about the projects you have listed as you read through this section.*

Some service projects respond to specific needs that involve individuals or groups. Students can provide holiday meals for less- fortunate families in their community or make lunches on a regular basis for the homeless. They can collect items for individuals or families. These items can include coats, gloves, or shoes for needy families; books for children in low income child-care centers; and food for families who live at or below the poverty level.

## Supporting Local Organizations

Projects that support local organizations can also range from small, short-term activities to year-long projects. Students might put together a team to participate in a run to benefit a local cause, or commit to a year-long collaboration with a local organization by volunteering on-site on a weekly basis. Students might "adopt" a zoo animal and provide the money necessary to feed that animal for a year, or as in the story that follows, students can organize a school-wide canned food drive to support a local food bank.

In this book's Appendix (pages 65-73), are examples of service projects ranging from relatively small to more involved. They include *Coupons for All*, a *Mittens and Gloves Tree*, the school's *Lost and Found*, the *PTA Membership Drive*, a *Book Drive*, and a *Reading Service*. Each service project is described briefly. Suggestions are given for committees that could be formed to implement each project, as well as the responsibilities each committee would assume. Lists of possible work products for each project are also included.

# Summary

Service learning projects offer unique learning opportunities for elementary school students. The types of service projects for children are virtually limitless. Students can organize projects that meet needs within their school or within their community. While they learn the life-long skills of working with groups of people to implement plans, they also learn knowledge and skills of various content areas.

# The Story of One Service Project: A Canned Food Drive

When students are involved in service projects, their learning is rich and broad. They learn more than just the skills and information the teacher introduces. They become more competent people. This is the story of one service project, a canned food drive organized by first-grade students for their elementary school.

## The Canned Food Collection

On October 1, Terri, the principal of an elementary school, received an E-mail from the district office about the annual canned food collection. At most elementary schools, this announcement would be turned over to a PTA officer or a teacher committee. Adults would organize the drive for the school, and student involvement would be limited to bringing cans or boxes of food from home. But, things were done differently at this school.

**Note to the Reader**

*As you read this chapter, make notes about the types of learning the children engaged in as they worked through the canned food drive project. Look for their social development and personal growth, as well as the academic concepts and skills they learned.*

### Announcing the Need

There was an unwritten rule at this elementary school: adults do not do things that students are capable of doing and learning from. The principal jotted a note on an index card, "We just received information from the district about the annual canned food collection. If you are interested in organizing the drive this year, please write a note to Terri." She dropped the card in the News Crew folder. At this school, students made the morning announcements. Even the principal wrote out announcements she wanted to share with the school and turned them over to the News Crew. The next morning, a fifth grader on the News Crew read the principal's note over the public address system.

### Responding to the Need

After morning announcements, Claudia, a first-grade teacher, asked her students what they thought about taking on the canned food drive as a project. Most of the students had been in the school as kindergartners, were familiar with the canned food drive, and had an understanding of why the drive was important for people who did not have enough food. After a brief discussion, the class voted 20-2 to tell Terri that they would like to be responsible for this year's drive. The morning class meeting continued while Jessica and Christopher moved to the writing center to write a note to the principal.

Jessica slipped the note to Claudia. Claudia nodded, and without further comment, Jessica and Christopher walked to the office and put the note in the principal's box.

When Claudia picked up the mail in her box after lunch, there was a hand-printed note from Terri. Back in the classroom, Claudia showed the note to the class and read it aloud.

Then, Claudia read the district E-mail aloud to the class. They discussed what they thought some of the sentences meant and began dictating some notes on a chart tablet labeled "Things to Do." They took one more vote, which was 22-0 in favor of being in charge of the canned food drive, and decided to start planning the project the next afternoon.

## Planning the Work

The next day, Claudia opened the meeting by reading the list of "Things to Do" that the students began dictating the day before:

- Get lots of cans and boxes of food.
- Ask everyone to bring food.
- Collect food every day.
- Put all food in boxes.
- Take food to the Food Bank.

These were jobs that children had dictated from their understanding of the district memo. Now, it was time to expand the list and begin deciding how to complete each item on the list. Claudia asked the class how they thought they could "get lots of cans and boxes of food." When one student responded, "We already said that. Ask everyone to bring food," Claudia pushed a little, "Okay, so how are we going to do that?" There was a moment of silence, so Claudia asked students to pair up and talk about how the class could ask for food. After a few minutes of talking together, different students dictated ways to ask families in the school to donate food to the drive:

- Write a letter.
- Make morning announcements.
- Call every family.
- Make signs and put them in every hall.
- Send E-mails.
- Talk to each class.

Dear, Terri.
we wood lik to do the can fod drif.
claudias clas

*Letter to Terri (principal)*

Dear Claudia's class,

I received your note volunteering to organize the Canned Food Drive for our school this year. This is an important job. The schools in our district need to collect as much food as we can to help the people in our city who do not have enough to eat. It will be a lot of work. I know you can do it if you want to, but I want to make sure that you understand everything that is required. Attached is a memo from the school district. Please read it and ask Claudia any questions you have. Then take another vote to make sure this is something the class wants to do.

Terri

*Letter to Claudia's Class*

## Expanding the Focus

These were all methods of communication that students had used in other projects. Claudia did not want her students to be content with just using methods that they had tried before. To get them thinking more broadly, she brought up the idea of talking to "experts" about canned food drives. "You guys have come up with a good list. But, I wonder if we should talk to some people who know a lot about asking for donations. What do you think about interviewing some students who were in charge of last year's canned food drive? What about some of the PTA officers who ask for other kinds of donations from the families of our school? What about people who work at the food bank? Is there anyone else we know who might answer our questions or give us advice?" In response to each suggestion, the students agreed that it would be a good idea to talk with the people mentioned. With some additional prompting by Claudia, one child mentioned that his father asked for donations at their church, and another child said that his mother asked for donations to buy their T-ball coach a present. These two parents were added to the list of "experts" that the class would consult.

## Sharing the Work

Within minutes, students had volunteered to work on different committees related to seeking advice from other people. One group would identify students who organized last year's drive and find out which classes they were in this year. Two students would get the PTA president's telephone number from the school secretary. They would call her to get the name and number of the officer who was in charge of fund-raising. They would prepare for their phone call by filling in the Phone Call Planning sheet (page 76). Students would use this form to record the results of their calls as well. Two other students were ready to call the food bank to find out who they should talk to. The two students who had parents who asked for donations agreed to interview their parents at home. The other students divided into three groups to work on interview questions for students, the PTA officer, and food bank staff.

Over several days, during project time, students worked in committees to interview experts; work out the logistics of collecting and sorting the cans and boxes of donated food; and draft the morning announcements, letters, signs, and advertising posters (pages 77-78).

## Interviewing the "Experts"

Interviews with the "experts" expanded the children's thinking about how they would conduct their canned food drive. The students who had been in charge of last year's canned food drive offered several suggestions about organizing the drive. The director of the food bank provided several "facts" about the work of the food bank that the students could include in their letters and morning announcements. The vice president of the PTA agreed to put an article in their monthly newsletter asking families to support the canned food drive. She also suggested that students try to get everyone in the school to ask people outside of the school for donations. She said that they could

1. How much food did you get
2. How meny letters did Send hom
3 Did you Call peel
4. Did you mak sins?
5. What is did you do?

*Interview Questions for Students*

get much more food if students asked their relatives, neighbors, and family friends. These "experts" were all helpful, but the person who challenged the children's thinking the most was Jorge's father.

Jorge's father, a minister on staff at a large local church, solicited donations at his church. Among his responsibilities was raising money for special church projects. After talking to his son, he agreed to talk to the class about fund-raising issues that he considered important. In a brief presentation, he explained that it was more effective to ask people in person rather than sending letters. He said that he always tells people why their gift is important and what their donation will make possible. He also explained pledges to the class, telling them that a pledge is a letter saying that a person will give a certain amount in the future. The class followed his presentation with a short meeting. After discussing options, they decided that it would be too hard to meet with all of the families in the school, but they could talk to parents who brought their children to school in the mornings or picked them up in the afternoons. They set up another committee to work on a speech they could give parents when they talked to them. Each committee kept their own lists of responsibilities and used these lists for reporting to the class during the class's daily check-in meetings. The students used the Committee Task Sheet (page 79) to record each responsibility, the student in charge of each task, and the deadline for each job.

## Beginning the Drive

Within two weeks, the canned food drive was launched. A pair of students made a presentation to each class in the school, and students were given small information cards to use when talking to their parents, relatives, neighbors, and friends about the canned food drive. A letter was distributed to each family in the school, and each student received a card-stock reminder with an attached magnet to put on the family refrigerator. Students displayed posters advertising the drive beside every classroom in the school. Groups of students were in charge of talking to parents before and after school each day. The children created a bar graph for the classroom and hung a large thermometer graph near the school's office (see pages 80-81). Students updated both graphs daily.

## Collecting the Food

Teachers received memos asking them to remind students to place donations in the halls outside their classroom doors before 9:30 A.M. Claudia's students paired, and each pair took on the responsibility for counting the donations from different classes and bringing them back to their own classroom. Charts and lists of the food collected seemed to fill the classroom. This was a lot of planning for six- and seven-year-old children, but they had help along the way from the "experts" that they interviewed and from Claudia.

> Dear Families:
>
> Lots of people in our city do not have enough money to buy food. We can help them if we share some of our food.
>
> These families need all kinds of food. We will give the food we get to the Food Bank and they will give the food to families. People who work at the Food Bank say there are more families who need help than last year.
>
> For three weeks, our class is going to go to every room and get the food that families send in. We hope you will send cans and boxes of food to school soon. We hope you will ask other people you know to give food too.
>
> Thank you,
>
> Claudia's Class

*Letter to Families #1*

## Proceeding Day-to-Day

The classroom itself was rearranged, and different parts of the room were labeled milk group, meat/protein group, vegetables, fruits, cereals/pasta/rice group, and desserts. When each student pair returned to the room with donated food, they recorded the numbers on a chart near the computer, then sorted the food. Two children volunteered to count that day's donations by food groups. That number was recorded on a different chart near the computer, and later that day, a committee of children compared the two charts to make sure the numbers were the same.

## Making Observations about the Collection

Every day of that week, students in Claudia's class performed the same collecting and counting jobs. In their morning meeting on Friday, Michael made the comment that there were "lots and lots of vegetables, but almost no cans of meat." The class had studied the food pyramid when they created the way to sort the food. As a part of the project, they discussed balanced meals, and for a week, they compared the school's lunches to the food pyramid. Claudia listened to Michael and a few other students talk about how people who go to the food bank cannot balance their meals if most of what they choose from is canned vegetables. Considering how she could best direct their conversation and expand their learning, Claudia commented, "I wonder how we could find out if this is a problem for the food bank or if this is just something happening in our school's food drive." That sentence was enough to prompt the students who had interviewed the director of the food bank earlier in the project. They decided to call the director and ask more questions.

In their next class meeting, the girls reported that the director of the food bank told them that vegetables were very important to balanced meals, but they had lots of vegetables in stock, and donated food was usually short on selections from the meat/protein and fruit groups.

## Solving the Problem

Claudia asked the class what they thought they should do, and Michael said that his committee had discussed this the day before and wanted to write a letter to families. "How can families send in foods we need if they don't know what we already have?" That afternoon, his committee drafted a letter, received principal approval to send it home to families in the school, copied the letter, and distributed copies to all classes.

Beginning the next morning, the donations of canned foods increased, and the majority of cans came from the meat/protein and fruit groups. The children were elated the next afternoon when the day's count and running totals were announced. They realized that they had made a difference in the kinds of donations that were being sent in.

Dear Families,

A lot of families have sent food to school. Thank you.

We have a lot of cans of vegetables. People at the Food Bank say they need more canned meat and canned fruit.

Please send some of these cans if you can. Please ask friends and family to send some food for the canned food drive. People need our help.

Thank you,

Claudia's Class

*Letter to Families #2*

Morning announcements continued. Children continued their daily visits to collect food stacked in the halls outside classroom doors. Students counted the donations and made entries on the correct charts.

## Ending the Drive

By the final day of the canned food drive, Claudia's class had more than 4,162 cans and boxes of food to donate to the food bank. They were excited that they had collected more food than the year before. They seemed overwhelmed with the amount of food in the classroom. (Cans and boxes of food had almost taken over the room!) They were pleased that they changed the types of canned food that families were donating so that there was as much meat/protein and fruit as vegetables.

## Summary

This narrative chronicles one service learning project. It gives an idea of how one such project might evolve from a class deciding to take on a service project to its culmination.

Service projects are valuable in and of themselves because they benefit others. However, most elementary teachers do not have time for activities just because they are "good." There are simply too many concepts and skills that students must learn at each grade level. However, with proper planning on the teacher's part, a significant number of concepts and skills can be learned within the context of projects.

### Note to the Reader

*Before you turn the page, take a moment to look through your list of what the students learned, then compare your list to the following list created by the teacher of this first-grade class.*

# Knowledge and Skills Embedded in the Canned Food Drive Project

## Processes used throughout the project:

- planning and working as team members
- working independently
- using multiple resources
- helping others find resources
- setting work priorities
- allocating time
- brainstorming ideas and options
- negotiating solutions and decisions

## Class planning meetings:

- dictating lists of things to do
- making group decisions about priorities
- determining committees to be responsible for portions of the project
- volunteering for committee work
- holding "check-in" meetings to determine if committees are completing their work

## Creating announcements for the school public address system:

- determining the most important information
- noting important facts
- dictating scripts
- evaluating scripts for revisions
- using "reading" or reading-like behaviors to "read" scripts
- repeating readings to check voice quality, expression, etc.

## Memos, letters, and reminder notes:

- using letter-sound correspondence to spell words
- blending sounds to create words
- putting spaces between words
- using uppercase letters as needed
- following formats of memos, business letters, and friendly notes
- determining audiences for memos
- listing pertinent information only
- deleting unnecessary information or correcting mistakes

Service Learning Projects for Elementary Students • CD-104032 • © Carson-Dellosa

- consulting classroom resources for spelling help
- using a calendar as a resource for writing dates

## Doing peer response:
- using letter-sound correspondence to spell words
- following the conventions of writing
- writing on successive days

## Creating advertising posters:
- evaluating adult models for characteristics
- planning words for posters
- organizing first drafts of posters
- asking for peer response
- revising posters
- creating final posters

## Developing and meeting collection schedules:
- listing all teachers
- assigning pairs to classrooms
- determining pickup times
- borrowing wagons and rolling carts
- communicating the pickup schedule to teachers

## Counting cans and boxes:
- counting by classroom
- dividing day's contributions into categories
- counting by category
- comparing two counts to check accuracy

## Maintaining charts:
- following directions
- transferring hand counts to chart format
- printing daily reports

## Creating large graph and thermometer graphs to announce running totals:
- using rulers and yardsticks
- counting by multiples of 5 and 10
- transferring data from charts to graphs

## Preparing donations for food bank:

- boxing similar food types
- sealing and labeling donation boxes

## Self-evaluation:

- dictating what they have done to help with the project
- determining criteria for judging work and work habits

# Characteristics of Projects

Project-based learning is different from more traditional approaches to elementary learning. In a traditional class, the lessons are generally based on content-specific textbooks. The teacher makes decisions about what content and skills will be taught. Students listen to the teacher's presentation of the content, watch a demonstration of how to apply a particular skill, and then individually complete an assignment directly related to that lesson. While the children participate in activities that include them in lessons, they do not direct the lessons or make any decisions related to content.

In projects, the teacher and students take on slightly different roles. Mandated skills are still taught, but they are taught in a different manner. In a project-based classroom, children are involved in decisions about what they learn. They plan what course their learning will take, and they consult multiple resources along the way. They are encouraged to approach their work the way that professionals do. That is, students conduct research like scientists, gather data like researchers, and report facts like journalists. Additionally, they inform classmates and the teacher the way coworkers inform each other—in class meetings, by corresponding with memos, by presenting progress summaries to the group, by recording progress on flow charts, etc. This classroom environment is collaborative rather than teacher-directed.

All projects have certain characteristics in common. True projects:
- are student directed
- are research based
- consult multiple resources
- are connected to the real world
- are embedded with knowledge and skills

### Note to the Reader

*Because projects must include the five characteristics of being:*
1. *student directed,*
2. *research based,*
3. *informed by multiple resources,*
4. *connected to the real world,*
5. *embedded with knowledge and skills,*

*it is sometimes helpful to document how a project you are considering fulfills each characteristic. See page 82 for a form to help you document this information.*

Each characteristic brings an added dimension to students' learning. While each characteristic is important in its own right, when combined, all characteristics make for powerful learning.

## Student Directed

In project-based learning, students make more decisions about their learning than many other elementary children. Many teachers consider themselves and their classrooms to be "child-centered." But, project-based teachers carry that idea further and create "student-directed" classrooms.

Students make many initial decisions about what projects the class will undertake. With the teacher's support and guidance, the whole class begins initial planning for a project. Then, on a day-to-day basis, individuals and small groups of children decide what they will accomplish during project time that day. Students are actively engaged in the project and in their learning. Students who make decisions about what they do in school have a deeper investment in their learning.

## Note to the Reader

*If you have been teaching in a teacher-directed way in which you have made all decisions about learning experiences in your classroom, this may be the most difficult project characteristic to implement. Allowing students to make decisions means giving up some control and may be outside of your comfort zone. Perhaps a first step toward creating a student-directed class would be to come up with two or three options, that you could "live with." Then, let students decide among those options. As you observe what your students learn, especially related to problem solving and decision making, you will see the value in student-directed learning and become more comfortable allowing students to make decisions.*

Thinking back to the narrative of the canned food drive project (pages 10-18), it is easy to see the decisions that students made about their work in that service project. The students in Claudia's class decided to accept the responsibility of organizing the canned food drive for the school. They considered the principal's request and voted to take on the canned food drive as a class project. As their teacher, Claudia would have accepted a negative vote as readily as she did their commitment. If she felt strongly that the students needed this particular experience, she might have shared her reasons for wanting them to do this project, but if her reasoning failed to convince them, she would have accepted their rejection.

With her guidance and pondering way of leading students, Claudia's class made decisions about how to start the project. Initial planning for a project frequently begins as it did in the canned food drive project, by making a list of "Things to Do." Later, the list is rearranged in priority order, according to responsibilities of different committees, or in a time-specific manner.

By making individual decisions about their project work, Claudia's students volunteered for jobs related to the canned food drive. Some jobs were one-day tasks, such as being a partner who called the PTA president to find out which officer was in charge of fund-raising. Other jobs might continue throughout the project, such as serving on the committee to maintain the daily running totals for donated cans and boxes of food.

As problems or differences of opinions arise during projects, students brainstorm possible solutions to each problem and decide what solution they will try first. For example, if students begin arguing about who will make morning announcements, Claudia can end that argument with, "Stop arguing. Jason and Breanna will make the announcements because they are not arguing." That will end the conflict, and the decision about who will make the announcements will be made. But, as a project-based teacher, Claudia would not do that. If she does, student learning will be stifled. She recognizes that conflict is a natural part of any group project. By getting the students who were involved in this conflict to identify the problem, think about possible solutions to it, and give reasons for what they each wanted, Claudia can support children's learning about how to solve problems.

Student-directed does not mean that students have absolute freedom. Students cannot do just any project they dream up or make random decisions. Project teachers do not passively allow students to make bad decisions. They do not relinquish their responsibilities to teach in the name of supporting student-directed projects. Teachers in project-based classrooms equate children learning to make good decisions with the importance of learning any other skill. Students need to be taught how to make good decisions and need to have many opportunities to make increasingly complex decisions.

While students make decisions throughout the course of a project, these decisions are based on the needs and outcome of the project as well as the learning involved. Conducting research becomes very important in project-based learning.

## Research Based

Because children in project-based classes approach their work like professionals, research takes on added importance. Project-based teachers encourage children to seek answers to questions and help students learn the research skills necessary to carry out their work. In many schools, the research conducted by students is related to answering content-specific questions. In project-based classes, content is not the only thing students research.

**If . . . Then**

*If you cannot find sufficient resources related to your class project, then consider these actions: send a letter to students' families asking for suggestions; send a memo to other teachers in your school asking if they know of written resources or people who know about your project's topic; locate a person in your community who is knowledgeable about your project's topic and ask for resource suggestions.*

Claudia's students were taking on a responsibility that was new to them. They had never organized any kind of drive, so they did not have personal experiences to draw from. One of the first things they did was "research" how to conduct a canned food drive. They began the project by interviewing students who had been in charge of the canned food drive the year before, as well as talking with PTA officers and staff at the local food bank. Further, some students conducted additional research about how professionals raise money by talking with a parent who sought donations as part of his job.

Claudia could have told students how to conduct a canned food drive. She could have assumed the responsibility herself, then assigned small tasks to her students every day. But Claudia, as most teachers in project-based classrooms, believes that students learn more when they direct their own learning. Conducting good research not only answers student questions, it is also the basis for making good decisions about learning.

Just because projects are research-based, and students conduct that research, project teachers do not take passive roles in this process. Teachers teach students to conduct research. They show them what to do with the information they learn. They ensure that students have resources in sufficient quantity and quality to be successful in their research. Teachers guide students by asking probing, even leading, questions.

Students in project-based classes are encouraged not to rely on information from a single source, even if it is a textbook or teacher. Students are taught to look for information from multiple resources, preferably different types of resources.

## Multiple Resources Consulted

One important message that project-based teachers communicate to their students is that textbooks are not the only resource for learning. Too much learning in elementary school classrooms focuses on what textbooks say. In the real world, very few answers are found in a single resource. Project-based teachers want students to go beyond textbooks and become familiar with different types of resources.

Multiple resources include written texts (books, magazines, journals, brochures, pamphlets, etc.), Internet sources, interviews with people who know about the topic being investigated, and observation. For example, in the canned food drive, children studied the food pyramid to obtain information about a balanced diet. Students observed how the food bank stores and distributes food while reading informational texts about food and nutrition. Some families contributed articles from health magazines, and a small group of children interviewed food bank staff to find out what foods were most popular with clients and what foods the food bank needed the most.

As students consult multiple resources, their research takes on an added dimension. They learn more than they would from a traditional text. They begin to realize how their school learning is applied in the world and see a reason to master class work. They become actively involved in their work and not only learn required information, but also how to approach a real problem and gather information about it.

## Connected to the Real World

Service projects are related to events in the world outside of the classroom. Service projects are authentic learning experiences in which children participate actively in their learning. Throughout projects, students emulate ways that adults accomplish work in the real world.

Children consult adult models for examples about how to conduct their business. In the canned food drive project, the children sorted canned and boxed goods using the same system as the food bank. In the Coupons for All project (page 65), kindergarten children copy the way informational brochures are displayed, constructing a similar arrangement from envelopes and poster board. Young children's work will not reach the sophistication of adult work, but children can practice the approaches that professionals use.

If the project calls for children to create a newsletter, they should consult newsletters produced by adults or older children. When they need to make a poster, they should look at professional posters displayed in the school or in nearby businesses. When they need to advertise their services, they should consult newspaper ads, magazine spreads, or direct mail pieces.

Projects come from needs in the real world, and they are completed for a reason. Projects further student learning and have deep roots in necessary knowledge and skills.

# Embedded with Knowledge and Skills

As they complete a service project, children also master knowledge and skills that are integral parts of their education. They learn to write letters, formulate questions to get answers they need, record pertinent information, devise systems that accomplish tasks, etc. They meet government requirements for reading, writing, math, science, social studies, and fine arts. But, they are doing it through a different type of curriculum, through authentic tasks that are parts of project-based learning.

When children work on projects, it is easy for teachers to embed reading and writing standards. Students read to gather information, and write to document what they learn. In addition, students write when they create plans for the project and produce products such as letters, flyers, advertising posters, etc. Teachers can take virtually any reading or writing objective and teach it in the context of project work. For mathematics, counting, measuring, and graphing can be worked into almost any project. Embedding objectives related to science and social studies may take more thought, but it can be done.

## If . . . Then

*If you are having difficulty determining which standards and objectives to work into a service project, then try listing the possible work samples that will be part of the project. List skills that students need in order to produce that work. From this list of skills, reading and writing standards and objectives should be easy to identify. To identify math, science, or social studies standards and objectives, talk with a colleague. Talking through a project usually helps identify different possibilities.*

Working in project-based situations reinforces the notion that learning is done for a reason, not just because it is on a page of a textbook. When students see the need for learning a particular skill, they are more inclined to really learn it. Within the context of a project, students use the skills they learn to accomplish a particular task. When they immediately apply new knowledge or a new skill, they tend to remember it, instead of just memorizing it for an end-of-week test.

In the canned food drive project, Claudia's students counted the number of collected cans, packaged them in multiples of 10, and graphed the results for the school to see. State mandates require that these skills be taught. The students wrote letters to various audiences: to the principal asking about conducting the drive, to the food bank to inquire about their procedures, and to families in the school to request donations. They kept daily logs of their achievements, making notes about what was accomplished and what still needed to be done.

# Summary

It is evident that students learn much more than facts as they plan and implement projects. Students gain required knowledge and skills as teachers embed knowledge and skills into projects. Students learn decision-making and problem-solving skills as they direct projects. They learn how to learn as they consult multiple resources to research various aspects of each project. And, because projects are always connected to the real world, students discover how to use what they are learning in situations beyond the classroom.

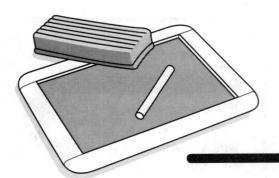

# The Project-Based Classroom

Project-based-learning classrooms share several characteristics. They are busy, active places where children work in different groupings. Collaboration occurs frequently as children are encouraged to work together, talk, share, negotiate, and solve problems. Students gather the materials and supplies needed to support their daily work. The classroom is arranged to enhance the work that goes on in these groups.

In most project classrooms, there is a meeting area large enough for all children to gather for class meetings, and desks or tables are grouped together to encourage small group work. The necessary materials are located where all students can easily access them. Pencils and markers can be stored in a basket on each table or group of desks; a variety of paper is kept in a writing center; and glue, scissors, and other supplies are stored so that children can reach them. Children also have free access to resource materials. Dictionaries and thesauruses are located on low shelves, and at least one student computer (with Internet access and a CD-ROM encyclopedia disk nearby) is located in a private area of the classroom. The implementation of project-based learning begins with the organization of the classroom, especially meeting areas.

## Meeting Areas

Project work requires that students meet as a whole class, that small groups collaborate, and that individuals have spaces to work independently. Each type of group requires a different configuration of space. So, the arrangement of furniture in the classroom must offer various areas to accommodate different groupings of students. While each area meets unique needs of different groupings, the spaces blend together to create a balanced classroom.

The whole-group area needs to be large enough so that all students in the class can sit together. Most classes simply sit on the floor. The whole-group meeting area is often defined by a rug or set off by couches. This area is usually located adjacent to one wall of the classroom so that there is easy access to a chalkboard or white board. An easel is also placed nearby to hold chart paper for recording class discussions or decisions. A basket, or other similar container, should be easily accessible to the meeting area. This basket is used to store necessary supplies that are often needed during group meetings, items such as markers, scissors, tape, highlighting tape or markers, note pads, etc.

### If . . . Then

*If the classroom is too small to designate a large enough space for a whole-group meeting area, then students may need to move desks each day to create this space. While moving desks each time you have a whole-group meeting is not desirable, it is better than trying to hold class meetings in a space that is too small. When children cannot sit comfortably, it inevitably leads to conflicts among students.*

24

Areas where small groups meet vary from classroom to classroom, depending on the configuration of the room and the preferences of students and the teacher. Students may use their regular seating areas in the classroom. Tables can double as small-group meeting places, or desks can be rearranged to allow work spaces for small groups. However, it usually works better if students have options. Some children prefer to work on the floor, using clipboards or other hard surfaces as work spaces. Working on the floor works well for elementary-aged children. It extends their work space, allowing room to spread out materials as needed. Small groups can meet in each corner of the classroom and in the whole-group meeting area. Not only does this give all groups room to spread out as needed, but it disperses the noise associated with small-group work.

## If . . . Then

*If the easel is too high for children to see when they are sitting on the floor, then lower it. Lowering the shelf that holds the chart or shortening the legs moves the chart to a lower level. This also places the chart at the children's level so that they can write on it easily.*

Students also need spaces where they can work individually. These spaces can be as obvious as a seat at a table or a desk pulled away from the group. However, some children prefer to work in a "private space." That might be a private corner of the classroom, under a table, or in the hall (if that is permitted in your school).

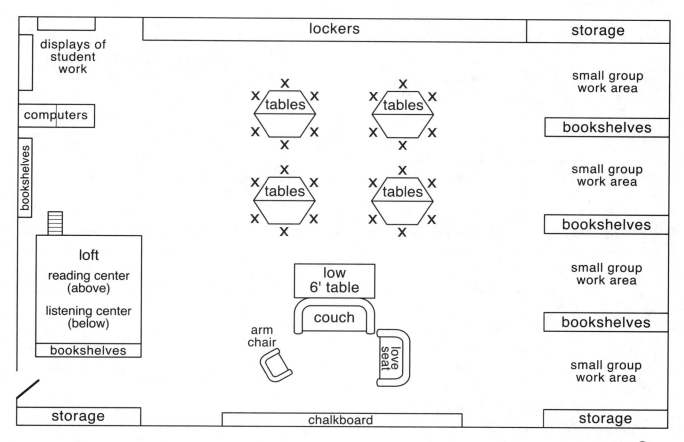

Obviously, there is no single, "right" way to arrange a classroom to support project-based learning. There are too many variables that affect how teachers set up classrooms: size of the classroom; configuration of the room; available furniture; and placement of windows, chalkboard, bulletin boards, lockers, or cubbies. This diagram of a classroom (page 25) shows one way to ensure that the arrangement of the furniture supports different groupings of students and that supplies, resources, and student work are easily accessible.

## Classroom Arrangement

Examine your classroom with the requirements of project work in mind and ask yourself the following questions:

1. Is the whole-group meeting area large enough so that all students can sit comfortably?
2. What can you do to designate the whole-group meeting area? Add a rug? Define the area with bookshelves?
3. Are there several small-group areas in different parts of the classroom?
4. Do you need clipboards for students to use if they work on the floor?
5. Are there any "privacy" areas for children to work alone? If not, can some be created by rearranging furniture?

**If . . . Then**

*If students are accustomed to having their own personal supplies, then have a class meeting to introduce the idea of shared supplies. Explain your reasons for wanting to use shared supplies, then ask how students feel about sharing supplies. Ask students to suggest places to locate different types of supplies. Then, involve the class in setting up the areas where supplies will be stored.*

If you believe that you could rearrange your classroom to better support project work, experiment with different placement using the reproducible grid (page 94).

## Supplies

In project-based classrooms, sharing supplies works well. When children negotiate how to share supplies, they develop a stronger sense of community and learn necessary negotiating skills. This adds to the collaborative nature of projects.

While it is difficult to predict all supplies that children might need during the course of a project, some general supplies are usually necessary. These supplies include:

- pencils, standard and colorful
- pencil sharpeners
- pens, felt-tip and highlighting
- paper, in a variety of sizes, colors, lined, and unlined
- felt-tip markers, crayons, and chalk
- brushes and paint
- rulers, yardsticks, and measuring tapes
- staplers and staple removers

- scissors, tape, glue, and glue sticks
- hole punches, single and three-hole
- date stamp and stamp pads

These shared supplies can be located in different parts of the classroom: on each table, in each learning center, and/or in any easily accessed area of the classroom.

Other supplies that children might need include a die-cut machine or a set of letter stencils for making letters to create signs, laminating supplies to protect certain work, and book binding supplies, such as thread, needles, paper fasteners, or, if possible, a binding machine and spines. Easy access to a photocopying machine is also helpful.

Students must be taught where supplies are located, what the expectations about using the supplies are, and what the class routines are for accessing and returning supplies to the "places where they belong." For younger children, it is important to remember that telling them the expectations about using shared supplies is not sufficient. Early childhood teachers model how to get supplies and return them to their proper places. They also engage the children in role-playing these routines to help them remember how to use supplies correctly. For example, demonstrate how a person walks to the pencil basket, selects a pencil, and returns to work. With older children, it may be sufficient to call attention to the locations of the materials. However, all students benefit from labeled storage areas (using picture labels for the youngest students) as a reminder about where different supplies are stored.

When shared supplies are used in a classroom, it is a good idea to ask students to share the responsibility of monitoring the supplies. Many teachers post a Supplies List (page 84) near the area where supplies are stored. As a student notices that one type of supplies is "getting low," she makes a note of that item on the supplies list. Students also note types of supplies that are not normally kept in the classroom but that they will need in the next few days, such as poster board, large chart paper, and so on. Maintaining this list helps the teacher remember what kinds of supplies she needs to purchase and prevents wasted time when students do not have the supplies they need to complete a particular task.

> **Note to the Reader**
>
> *If you are not currently using shared supplies in your class, you may need to acquire containers to hold the different supplies necessary for project work. Make a list of what you will need: stacking trays for different types of paper; plastic containers with lids for scissors, tape, glue, and glue sticks; plastic cups for markers, crayons, and pencils; etc.*

## Resources

During the course of a project, students need frequent access to reference materials, such as books, magazines, catalogs, etc. These materials, like supplies, should be located so that children can access them without an adult's assistance. Just having the resources is not enough; understanding where these resources are located and how to use them are important also. For example, if dictionaries are located in the classroom, the children must be taught that "this is the shelf where our dictionaries are kept" and reminded that "in this class, we always put books on a shelf with spines out."

Organizing written materials in a classroom can be a daunting task. While it is almost impossible to have too many books, magazines, and brochures, organizing them for easy access is a challenge. Possible solutions include grouping them into categories or arranging them by author. Books and other written materials that are used to support a particular project should be stored in a separate area in the classroom away from the class library. Project-related resources can be stored in magazine holders, crates, baskets, or plastic tubs. Whatever the choice of storage container, these materials should be organized and labeled.

Various technologies also serve as project resources. Access to word processing-programs or Internet connections for e-mailing or research is helpful. Necessary CDs or disks should be located near the computer.

Resources for project work also include class lists of "things to do," reminders about problems that need discussing, questions that committees have for the class, and other charts. These are written on chart paper or poster board in easy-to-read handwriting. They should always be hung low enough so that students can access them.

**If . . . Then**

*If your school does not provide all of the supplies mentioned in this section, or other specific supplies that will be needed for a particular project, then share the list with students' families and ask for donations of these items to the class. Families are often generous when they are aware of a class's needs.*

While the resources mentioned previously are general, certain service projects require particular resources. For example, if a class is organizing a canned food drive for the entire school, project committees may need to locate statistics about the number of families in the school's community that do not have resources to buy enough food for their families or different foods that represent each part of the food pyramid. Project teachers often provide forms for students to document the resource or the type of information they need to complete their part of the project. A committee fills out the Request for Resources Form (page 85) and posts it in a prominent place in the classroom so that students who are not on that committee can be aware of the need. Completing the form formalizes the request for assistance, so that other students, or the teacher, can help locate the necessary resources.

## Student Work

As students work through a project, it is important to teach them various ways to organize their research or planning documents. Depending on the complexity of the task, a simple file folder system works well. Give each child a folder for storing his work and show him how to label it clearly. Then, file folders can be stored in a filing cabinet. Pocket folders can also be used. They have pockets to hold smaller papers, as well as paper fasteners to hold three-hole punched papers. Other organizational aids include envelopes, fasteners such as paperclips or bulldog clips, expandable files, ABC files, dividers, three-ring binders, etc.

Some student work will not be kept by individual students. Some student work belongs to the entire class, such as the project calendar. Each project has its unique deadlines. Often, one task must be accomplished before another can take place. It is helpful to use class planning calendars to record due dates, deadlines, and/or other necessary information. Posting a wall-sized calendar or using a desk-style calendar on a bulletin board positions this information in a public place where all children can easily see it. Both calendar styles offer spaces to record daily information.

## Summary

For project work to be effective and efficient, the classroom itself needs to support that work. The furniture should be arranged so that it supports whole-group, small-group, and individual work. Supplies and resources should be organized and easily accessible to students. Supplies should be stored in accessible areas, and resources should be readily available. Organized systems should be developed to store student work. All of these elements support the success of project-based classrooms and, ultimately, project work.

**If . . . Then**

*If your students have not had previous experiences in organizing their own work, then you will need to teach them how to keep their project-related papers organized in the selected system. Younger students need explicit directions and practice on how to put papers in a file folder so that the papers do not extend beyond the folder. Older students may need directions about how to three-hole punch papers and insert them behind appropriate dividers.*

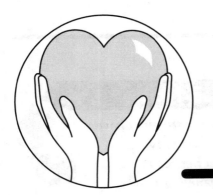

# The Project-Based Community

After the physical environment is arranged to support project-based learning, teachers can begin to think about the psychological environment of the class. They want their classes to feel safe, warm, and comfortable. Creating a community of learners among students is one way teachers ensure this feeling. Thus, creating a sense of community is a priority for project-based teachers at the beginning of every school year. Leading a group of elementary-aged students (who either do not know each other at all or have only a passing familiarity with each other) to come together as a learning community is not easy. But, establishing a cooperative community of learners makes life in the classroom so much richer. This sense of community is an important foundation for successful work in service projects.

Having a sense of community within a class means several different things. It starts with the classroom being a comfortable place for children but goes beyond that. In a class where community is emphasized, students often work independently and in small groups. They know each other well and care about each other. They learn to make decisions and solve their own conflicts, or at least solve them independently most of the time. Students do not come into a class at the beginning of a school year with these skills in place. Even students who have been in previous classes in which community was valued need opportunities to develop these skills with a new group of peers.

Students do not develop these skills on their own. Teachers work purposefully to teach students to work together in different groups, to care about each other and support each other's learning, to make group decisions, and to solve interpersonal problems and problems related to their school work. Teachers plan experiences and provide specific opportunities that help children develop these skills.

## Getting to Know Each Other

The first step in creating a sense of community is for students to get to know the other children in the class. A group of relative strangers meets on the first day of school. Depending on the grade level, the children may have been in class with some students in previous years. They may have a passing acquaintance with others or may be neighborhood friends. The teacher may have information about the children from other teachers or because they have taught siblings before. But, this prior knowledge is usually superficial. At the beginning of the year, teachers create multiple opportunities for students to truly get to know each other.

Some teachers spend a few minutes each day during the first week of school on getting-to-know-you activities. These activities are designed to give the teacher personal information about students and to get students to mix together in nonthreatening ways. Teachers often ask children to fill out surveys about their likes and dislikes or use some of the following activities:

- Two students interview each other, then each introduces his partner to the class.
- Each student brings an object that shows something about a personal interest and shares that with the class

Service Learning Projects for Elementary Students • CD-104032 • © Carson-Dellosa

in a show-and-tell format. (For example, a child who loves soccer might bring in a soccer ball, an avid game player a game, etc.)

- Students create and display personal posters by cutting out pictures from magazines and creating collages.
- Each student writes a poem that describes herself (page 86).
- In small groups, students play "Two Truths and a Fib" in which each student takes a turn making three statements about himself. Two statements are true and one statement is not true. The others in the group try to guess which statement is the "fib."
- As a whole class, students play Personal Interest Bingo (page 87).
- Students complete Thank-You Cards to recognize students who have done something helpful and post the completed cards on a bulletin board (page 88). A student might fill out a card that reads "Thanks to Jason for helping me find a book. Signed, Jody."

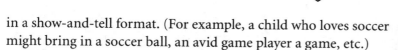

**If . . . Then**

*If students are not accustomed to recognizing specific acts of others and complimenting each other, then model this for them. Observe carefully. Several times during the day, recognize student behavior that is particularly helpful and share it with the class.*

Providing simple getting-to-know-you activities is just the beginning of creating a sense of community among students. Project-based teachers go beyond these activities. They want children to know each other, but they also want students to develop caring feelings for each other and establish working relationships.

Project teachers begin on the first day to turn decisions back to the students by modeling decision-making techniques, giving responsibilities to the students, and teaching children the value of good communication. In order to do this, teachers provide many situations in which students in different groupings work, make decisions, and create work products together. Working with different partners and in different small groups allows students to begin recognizing each other's strengths. They learn who is a strong reader, writes well, edits well, does mental math quickly and accurately, has creative ideas, draws realistic pictures, and so on. Over time, students come to realize that the teacher is not the only person in the classroom who knows the answers. They begin to see their classmates as capable people who can also help. When students need help in one of these areas, they know they can go to one of their peers for assistance. The teacher supports this by referring other students to them. This interdependence among students is a strong component of a class community.

Just as teachers encourage interdependence among students, adults also foster the sense that the class is "in this together" and that everyone helps each other. In class meetings, teachers often mention acts of kindness they have witnessed or point out ways that students help each other. This extends to the greater school community, as well. For example, the principal might consult small groups of students about issues that directly involve them or a committee of fifth graders might consult the PTA as they plan promotion activities.

## Developing a Caring Atmosphere

Teachers also create multiple opportunities at the beginning of the year for students to develop a caring attitude toward each other. Teachers do not insist that everyone in the class becomes friends; however, in creating a sense of community, teachers do require that students treat each other in respectful ways.

The development of a caring attitude begins as children observe the teacher's interactions with their classmates. As the teacher exhibits genuine concern and feeling for the children, they come to expect that from her. Her example leads the children to learn to care for each other. The teacher continually refers children to each other for help, saying "Kathleen, could you help James find his jacket?" when the teacher probably could find it more easily herself.

As that feeling is established, the teacher then helps children extend it to other children in the school. Suggesting that "our neighbors across the hall might want to share our soccer balls" or asking "Mrs. McGuire's class needs to go to lunch at our time today. Can we trade times?" encourages the children's caring attitude.

One of the first ways that teachers support the development of respectful relationships among the students in their classes is to treat children respectfully themselves. By using respectful language and a respectful tone of voice, teachers model how children should speak to each other in the classroom. Children tend to adopt the language that teachers show them.

Teachers also support respectful relationships among their students in more direct ways. In class meetings, teachers ask students to brainstorm respectful ways to use language in different situations that are common in elementary classrooms, for example, how to ask for something, how to ask for help, how to tell someone that he has done something you don't like, how to ask someone to stop an annoying behavior, etc. Some teachers introduce one issue at a time, such as how to ask someone to stop an annoying behavior, and ask students to list different comments that would show a respectful way to talk to other students about that one issue. They write the suggestions on chart paper and post these respectful language examples around the classroom. Other teachers present a list of common classroom statements that are not respectful and ask students to work together in pairs or small groups to come up with more respectful statements (page 89).

Beyond treating each other respectfully, teachers who value community in their classes encourage students to actively support each other. They talk about everyone having areas of strength and areas where they need help. Teachers reinforce the idea that everyone in the class can and should help others. Extending this feeling to the community through service projects is a natural progression. When children care for their classmates, this concern transfers to people outside the classroom.

**Strategies for Teachers**

*Some respectful language that project-based teachers use is:*

- *I noticed . . . .*
- *When you . . . , I feel . . . .*
- *Thanks to . . . for . . . .*
- *Everyone, notice how . . . did . . . for us.*
- *You . . . (tied your shoes, organized our books, etc.) by yourself. Thank you.*
- *You . . . (picked up trash, etc.) when you were not involved. Thank you.*
- *What a kind thing to do! You . . . when you . . . !*

## Establishing Routines

In a class where children are expected to help each other, make decisions, and solve problems, they need to know what behaviors are expected of them (Developmental Studies Center, 1996). A project-based teacher spends time with the children explaining and practicing the routines needed to help the class run smoothly. Since developing independence is a goal of project-based teachers, routines are established for the repeated interpersonal and academic behaviors of the class. When these routines are in place, the teacher does not repeatedly explain the task. Instead, the students understand the expectations of the routine and carry on with their work as practiced. These interpersonal routines apply to things such as establishing the morning routine for coming into the classroom or organizing how the lunch cards will be distributed. Some routines refer to the class's academic work. These might include the routine for selecting a book for independent reading time or working with a partner in a math game. Other academic routines can include how to get materials for a science experiment or how to replace supplies in a center.

The development of these routines does not come naturally to students. The teacher works with students during class meeting times to outline the desired routine, and the children spend time practicing and refining the routine until it meets their needs. Even after that, other class meetings are devoted to revisiting particular routines that are not going smoothly. But always, the teacher turns the responsibility of the decisions to the students as she holds them accountable for their behavior.

## Learning to Make Decisions

From the first day of school, teachers begin helping students make decisions. When students work on service learning projects, they cannot depend on the teacher to tell them what to do all of the time. Students are capable of making many decisions about their work but are often reluctant to make these decisions. More traditional teachers want students to follow their directions. After a year or two of school with traditional teachers, most students learn not to make decisions on their own but to check with their teacher before they do almost anything.

So, it often takes project-based teachers a few weeks to help students realize that they can make their own decisions, from small things, such as choosing among a pencil, a pen, or a marker for writing, to larger school issues, such as determining the class rules or choosing a service project for the class to undertake.

Teachers ask students to make many decisions but are careful only to offer options suitable to them so that they can live with the decisions that students make. Following are some examples of decisions that teachers might offer to elementary-age students:

- A teacher may ask a few students to choose what music to play in the classroom before announcements; however, he asks students to choose among CDs that he has placed near the CD player. This way he can be sure that all music chosen is appropriate for school.

### Note to the Reader

*Routines are directly related to class rules. Elementary-aged students are less likely to break rules when they have internalized class routines. There should be routines for common logistics such as what to do when:*

- *entering the classroom*
- *returning homework*
- *coming to the group area*
- *leaving the group area*
- *getting quiet*
- *taking turns talking*
- *following procedures for academic instruction*
- *getting necessary supplies*
- *lining up*
- *going to the lunchroom*
- *purchasing lunch and carrying it to a table*
- *cleaning up after eating*
- *moving to the playground*
- *gathering after recess*
- *preparing to go home*

- A teacher may ask two students to select one Tomie dePaola book for the morning read-aloud the week the class studies dePaola as their Author of the Week. In this case, it does not matter which book students choose. However, if the teacher had planned an activity based on *The Art Lesson* (Putnam Publishing Group, 1989), she would not offer this decision-making opportunity to students.
- A teacher may ask students whether they would prefer to have a morning or an afternoon recess time. However, if the school has a schedule for which classes can be on the playground at different times during the day, this is a decision that he would not offer.
- A teacher might ask the class to vote on whether they want to have independent reading time before lunch, after lunch, or at the end of the school day.
- A teacher can offer the class three different math games that all focus on the same math concept, then let children choose the game that they want to play.

Making good decisions is a learned skill. So, if teachers want students to make good decisions, then they must provide multiple opportunities for children to make decisions. Learning techniques for voting and reaching consensus are important to the class's development.

## Voting

Children can learn to indicate a vote by using simple hand signals, using the American Sign Language finger spelling of Y for yes and N for no, or they can record their votes using tally marks, etc. Younger children tend to vote for every option that is presented, so in those situations, it helps to suggest an action for everyone to do at the same time that indicates the vote. Suggesting that the "yes" voting people put their hands on their heads while the "no" voting people put their hands in their laps limits the number of times children can vote. Older children can use these techniques or use written voting methods. One way to record votes is to use a simple T-chart (see page 95 for Voting Chart). The teacher writes the question at the top of the page and labels the columns with possible answers. Each student then makes a tally mark under the column that fits her answer. It takes experimentation to find the simplest and most efficient way of voting for each group of children.

## Reaching Consensus

Teaching children how to reach consensus is the next step after learning to vote. Consensus is a good method to use when the situation does not call for an absolute vote. Consensus requires children to compromise; that is, even though they are not in total agreement with the class's plan, they agree to go along with it. It also indicates more cooperation; children indicate that they can cooperate with the class's decision, even though they do not completely agree. For example, when deciding how the playground equipment should

### If . . . Then

*Some young children have difficulty understanding the concept of voting and get very emotional when they lose a vote. If students react negatively to losing votes, then offer opportunities for the class to vote on issues that are less emotional. For example, for the morning read-aloud, allow the class to choose between two books. The book that gets the most votes is read right away. However, the book that gets the least number of votes will be read in the afternoon. In this type of vote, both sides win.*

be distributed and collected each day, suggestions are brought to the group and considered. Some children might feel strongly about having a "playground monitor" accept responsibility for the equipment, but others might feel just as strongly that each child who wants to play with the equipment should assume responsibility for what he uses. A teacher could explain consensus, asking the children in favor of a "playground monitor" to try the other method for a given length of time. After that time period, the class comes together again to see how the decision is working. This solution may be deemed the best one, other solutions may be suggested, or children may decide to try the alternate suggestion presented at the beginning. This process can continue until a suitable compromise is reached.

After explaining consensus, a project teacher might realize that most of the class is in favor of a particular decision and ask of dissenting children, "Even though it is not your favorite decision, can you go along with it?" When a sense of cooperation and turn-taking has been established, this system works smoothly.

## Leading but Not Telling

Teachers may know exactly what types of decisions they want students to make about classroom issues. They may know what kinds of rules they want in the classroom or how they want to arrange the daily schedule. They may know how they want class routines organized. But in classes where a sense of community is important, teachers do not make pronouncements about these issues. Teachers lead students to make these decisions. Project-based teachers typically use three different strategies to lead students to make certain decisions. These strategies are reflecting, pondering, and wondering aloud (Diffily and Sassman, 2002).

## Reflecting

In reflecting, teachers are careful not to add new information to the discussion. They make neutral statements, such as "Wow" or "Really?," or echo students' comments, such as "So, what you are saying is that you need to decide what color poster board to use for your signs" or "Hmm, you are trying to decide whether to use blue or yellow poster board." In this unbiased, reflecting manner of responding, teachers offer just enough support to help children make their own decisions.

Simply responding to children without making judgments is an effective technique to get students to analyze and clarify their thoughts. Some useful phrases include:

* Wow! I had not thought of that.
* Really? You're saying _____?
* Now what? Can you explain that to me again?
* I don't think Antwan heard you. Could you say that again?
* That's amazing!

## Pondering

When pondering, teachers model thinking more deeply about a particular question. Instead of directly answering a question that a student poses, teachers reply with a pondering-type response. The following questions are often used as teachers ponder:

- I'm not sure. Who could we ask?
- Do we know anyone who knows a lot about that topic?
- What do you think our options are?
- How could we do that?
- If that is what we want to do, what should happen first?
- Where do you think we might find something like that?

Obviously, these statements fit different situations. However, in each case, the teacher does not directly answer students' questions or solve their problem. Teachers encourage children to think more deeply about the issue and make their own decisions. Pondering puts the responsibility for decision making and learning back on students.

## Wondering Aloud

When wondering aloud, teachers are a bit more directive than in reflecting or pondering. With wondering aloud, teachers pose questions but offer more information than in the other two questioning strategies. Teachers direct students' thinking but do not tell children what to do. If a class has a question about caring for a certain plant and cannot find the answer, a teacher might wonder aloud, "I wonder if there is someone we could call who works at a place that sells that kind of plant. If he sells that plant, I'll bet he knows a lot about caring for it." Or, the teacher might say, "Another class of mine had this same problem. They voted to call the nursery where we bought the plant. I wonder if we could try that?" While teachers do not directly tell students what to do, they offer very specific suggestions for students to consider.

## Accepting Responsibility

One way to turn classroom responsibilities to the children is to develop class "experts." As soon as a child demonstrates a skill in a particular area or an interest in something, the teacher helps that child become proficient and names her "the expert" of that area. These jobs can be as simple as naming the child who can tie shoes as the "shoe-tying expert" in a kindergarten class or a bit more complex as in naming the upper elementary child who can debug the computer programs as the "computer expert."

Children also learn to take care of the materials in the class. Good project teachers hold children accountable for accessing and returning supplies to the correct places. Informal comments pointing out how "Agnes picked up a piece of trash even though she did not drop it" or how "John Robert returned the ball today without being reminded" establish the idea of accepting responsibility for actions.

## Learning to Communicate

To become good communicators, children must be taught to express themselves clearly, respond to others appropriately, and reflect on what they say or hear. Young children need explicit instruction to develop these skills, while older children need to refine and enhance skills they already have.

Getting children to work together in a successful manner also depends on establishing genuine concern among classmates. These children must be able to work together, share with each other, and treat others with respect. This does not happen without the guidance of adults. Involving children in service projects helps establish this

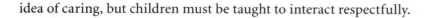

idea of caring, but children must be taught to interact respectfully.

As project teachers start the year, they teach children different ways to interact. In a class meeting, the teacher might set up situations in which children can practice interactions. As one person begins to talk, the teacher notes that "respectful listeners" turn their attention to the person speaking, suggesting that the children "turn your shoulders and face Richard so that he knows you are listening." They practice this skill over the next few days and continue practice throughout the year, as needed.

Teachers show children examples of how one comment relates to and builds on another comment. For example, Judith listens as Joy relates her opinion about a topic. Then, Judith tailors her comment to relate to Joy's comment. The teacher helps Judith learn to begin by saying, "Building on what Joy said, I think . . . ." The class can brainstorm ways to respond that show that good communication is occurring and record these ways on a chart for future reference.

The discipline system that is used in the classroom also sets the tone for positive interactions among children. Following models like *Positive Discipline* (Nelsen, 1996) encourages children to get along with and respect each other. Discipline models that call for one child's success at the expense of another's are not as useful. That is, if one child gets five stickers rewarding so-called good behavior and another gets none, the child who gets none is not particularly disposed to cooperate with the one who gets the rewards.

## Learning to Solve Problems

Just as making decisions is an important part of project work, so is solving problems. In an elementary school class, all kinds of problems arise that must be solved. Most problems in an elementary school classroom relate to conflicts among students or the work the children are doing. Most of the time, solutions are obvious to teachers. However, when teachers solve these problems, they are taking away students' opportunities to learn. Just as children need to make decisions to become good decision makers, they need to solve problems to become good problem solvers.

## Conflict Resolution

Conflict is inevitable when a group of people spend time together. A class of elementary school children is no exception.

**If . . . Then**

*If children have problems remembering who the experts are, then post a list of "Class Experts," determining a field of expertise for each student. These jobs are not spectacular accomplishments, rather they are the day-to-day details that help the classroom run smoothly. For example, the "stapler expert" knows how to refill the staples, the "tape recorder expert" can check the buttons to see that the correct ones are pushed, the "staple-puller expert" is adept at removing staples, etc.*

**If . . . Then**

*If your students have not had opportunities to solve their conflicts with peers, then you will need to teach them strategies to do this. You can offer five steps for resolving a conflict:*

*1. Define the problem.*
*2. Generate possible solutions.*
*3. Discuss each solution.*
*4. Choose one solution that all parties can agree to.*
*5. Evaluate the solution later.*

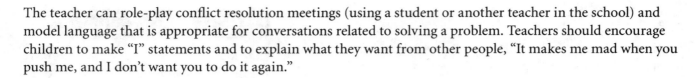

The teacher can role-play conflict resolution meetings (using a student or another teacher in the school) and model language that is appropriate for conversations related to solving a problem. Teachers should encourage children to make "I" statements and to explain what they want from other people, "It makes me mad when you push me, and I don't want you to do it again."

## Solving Work-Related Problems

All too often, elementary-aged students simply follow directions —underline, circle, put an X on, or choose from three possibilities—to complete their school work. Solving problems is an important skill that children can learn if they have the opportunity. In project work, children are faced with open-ended problems; those with no obvious answers or several possible solutions. Students must learn to approach these open-ended problems in logical, thought-provoking manners. Learning to solve work-related problems follows the same steps as solving interpersonal problems— state the problem, brainstorm a few solutions, then choose a solution.

Just as with interpersonal problems, project teachers support and guide children as they learn and practice the skill of problem solving. Teachers offer opportunities to role-play situations related to those they experience and revisit the practice as necessary.

**Note to the Reader**

*As you consider the issues raised in this chapter, think about ways you can create a sense of community among your students. Make notes, then prioritize the strategies you plan to use.*

# Summary

Creating a community of learners is the first step in preparing students to work collaboratively on projects. Learning to talk with each other respectfully, make decisions, and solve problems (both interpersonal and academic) leads students toward their first project.

Students are expected to master an extensive array of knowledge and skills before leaving elementary school. Because of this, if service projects were added to the required curriculum, it is unlikely that many elementary school teachers would have time to implement them while also presenting the necessary knowledge and skills required at their grade levels. However, many facets of the mandated knowledge and skills can be embedded into service projects, and students often learn these more quickly within the context of projects than they do when taught the same skills in isolation.

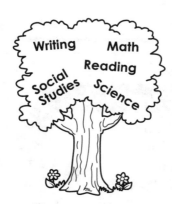

# The Academic Learning Embedded in Projects

Students tend to learn skills more quickly and remember knowledge they gain for longer periods of time when the knowledge and skills are embedded into the context of something they care about. Students almost always care, and care deeply, about their work in service projects. Within any service project, there are multiple opportunities for teachers to embed academic learning. Initially, it may take extra planning time, but within a relatively short period of time, embedding knowledge and skills into project tasks becomes almost second nature.

The following section offers specific suggestions for embedding academic knowledge and skills into service-learning projects. The five major disciplines taught in elementary school—reading, writing, math, science, and social studies—are discussed separately.

## Reading

Of all academic skills that children learn in elementary school, perhaps reading is the most important. Far from being a single skill, competent reading requires a number of skills that are learned through different methods of instruction: read-alouds, teacher modeling, direct instruction in large and small groups, guided practice, and independent practice. Teachers use a variety of materials to teach reading.

Project-related reading materials can be used to teach reading strategies and skills as easily as any other type of expository text. These reading materials might be magazine or newspaper articles, informational brochures, Web sites, flyers, letters, E-mail messages, labels, advertising, books, or anything that students read to research their project's topic. Any of these materials might be used to teach reading strategies or skills that students are ready to learn. Young students might be focusing on adding more high-frequency words to their sight word vocabularies or beginning to understand the structure of expository texts. Older elementary students might be learning how to skim texts for specific information or learning to differentiate between fact and opinion. Project-related reading materials add to the rich array of printed materials available in the classroom for students' reading choices.

Service projects provide a context for teaching reading skills in ways that engage children more deeply in the instruction. For example, when students receive a response to a letter they have sent, they are more likely to use

### If . . . Then

*If younger children are conducting the project, then it may be difficult to find articles, brochures, etc., written at the beginning reading levels. If this is the case, you can create informational brochures using simple sentence structure and vocabulary that your students already know. You can also teach children to use reading strategies they have learned to decode unfamiliar words, perhaps concentrating on captions for illustrations or labels.*

Service Learning Projects for Elementary Students • CD-104032 • © Carson-Dellosa

the reading strategies they are learning because they want to know what the letter says.

# Writing

Writing skills are readily integrated into project work because all service projects require different types of writing. As students engage in project work, they use writing to document what they learn through research. They write in many different formats as they create letters, brochures, and flyers that are part of the project. Other real-world types of writing can be taught to children and integrated into their service projects. These types of writing include:

- phone messages
- thank-you notes
- interviews
- supply lists of needed items
- reading recommendations related to the project's topic
- invitations and programs for project-related events
- résumés for project jobs or committees
- application letters for project jobs or committees
- procedural writing to document how to conduct a certain type of service project
- minutes of planning or check-in meetings
- school newspaper articles related to a project
- letters to families to inform school families about a project
- bulletin board announcements
- help-wanted postings

Different writing skills can be taught as children begin incorporating these types of writing into their project work.

As with learning reading skills, children also tend to pay more attention and work harder to learn writing skills when they need those skills to accomplish tasks during a project. Students also tend to remember these skills when they immediately apply them to a piece of writing that they have chosen to write.

When teaching project-related writing skills, teachers should remember to provide competent adult models of the type of writing students are learning about. If children are planning to write a business letter, teachers should share with them several authentic business letters and help them analyze the letters for common characteristics—format, language, etc. If students are creating advertising posters for a canned food drive, a PTA membership drive, or the school's lost and found, teachers should share commercially produced posters. Students can analyze

> **Note to the Reader**
>
> *Look through the state-mandated reading skills for your grade level. Put an asterisk beside each skill that could be taught using reading materials that might be used in a service project. Note that reading strategies related to expository text can most likely be taught during a service project.*

> **Note to the Reader**
>
> *Look through the mandated writing skills for your grade level. Put an asterisk beside each skill that could be taught using a type of writing that might be used during a service project.*

Der nesr WItolD)
TeS is the many
Tet we cldctet
for the por ceps
We hop it halPs
Tem
Fame coletts class

*Kindergarten Letter*

Dear Mrs. Hether,
The progect about
poinsettias is over but we
had a great time doing
the progect! We wanted
to thankyou for the
nice plants you let us
sale. I think our
costumers loved them dearly.
thankyou for your help.
          Sincerly,
          Joy's class

*Third Grade Letter*

these models, list characteristics of good advertising posters, and use that list to help create good posters. They typically produce higher-level work when they have competent adult work to use as models. That does not mean, however, that teachers should expect adult-quality work from elementary-age students. The business letters above are examples of grade-appropriate students' work that have been formed by examining competent adult models. Following is a translation of the kindergarten letter: *Dear Mr. Wild, This is the money that we collected for the poor kids. We hope it helps them. From Charlotte's Class*

Some people question the wisdom of asking elementary-age children to use adult models as guides for their own work. This practice would be inappropriate if children's work was expected to be the same quality as adult models; however, in any class there is a wide range of writing abilities. Teachers keep these abilities in mind as they work with individual children to emulate the given adult model.

Each time a model is presented to students with the suggestion that they use it to guide their own writing, there is also a wide range in the way that children produce their reproductions of that model. Very young children use scribbles in their efforts to reproduce a

## Strategies for Teachers

*Maintain files of competent models of different types of writing that might be used in a service project. Files might include business letters, letters to families, brochures, pamphlets, advertising flyers, advertising posters, proposals, invitations, magazine and newspaper articles, meeting minutes, event programs, résumés, etc. Check your state's writing standards to be sure you are collecting examples of every type of writing you are expected to teach.*

model, just as children who are in the next stage of writing will write random letters. That is acceptable. Teachers do not try to push children from one stage of writing to another or to pressure children to copy an adult's model. Instead, by using real-world models, children connect their school learning with the world outside the classroom. And, after all, preparing children for the real world is the purpose of teaching.

Helping young children examine adult models and identify good characteristics of those models is another way to scaffold children's writing. Scaffolding is the support a child needs to work at a level higher than she can work independently. Most of the time, scaffolding is provided by an adult or a more competent peer, but in some cases, a good model offers children the support that they need.

Genres written by adults are not the only models to use. Pieces of writing created by older students are just as effective. Teachers try to be aware of types of writing that students in the upper grades are learning during different times of the year. When fourth-grade students in the school are learning persuasive writing, project teachers might create a situation in which the younger students need to write a proposal for something. It might be to ask the principal if the class can use part of the playground for a vegetable garden or to ask students from other classes to donate books to a local children's hospital. Then, the fourth graders become the "experts" to teach the kindergarten or first-grade students about writing persuasively. This benefits both groups of students—the younger children get the benefit of more experienced learners, while the older students have opportunities to refine and revise their skills.

## Math

Math skills are required in most service projects. The particular math skills may vary from project to project, but typical skills used in project work include counting, adding, keeping a running total, subtracting, collecting and displaying data, comparing quantities, estimating, measuring, and keeping track of time. When students use these skills to create products that other people will see, they tend to learn the math skills more quickly and remember them for longer periods of time.

Some projects may not immediately seem to require math skills, but teachers can usually identify some way to include some math skills. In most projects, children can be asked to:

• maintain a class calendar of deadlines related to the project

- use time to create work schedules
- conduct a survey
- use survey data to create charts or graphs
- analyze data to draw conclusions or make decisions
- keep running totals (for example, number of people involved in the project, number of items collected, etc.)
- use computation to predict (For example, if we have __ items, and we need __ items, how many more items do we need?)
- use project-related items as open-ended word problems during math time
- use formulas to determine area or perimeter (for example, to determine how much grass seed is needed to plant in a particular area in a beautification project or how many plants, spaced 12" (30.5 cm) apart, are needed)

**Note to the Reader**

*If you are having difficulty figuring out how to integrate math skills into service projects students are working on, then speak with a math specialist in your district about the project. Sometimes an outside person can see a project with "new eyes." A math specialist may see opportunities for embedding different math skills in a project that you do not immediately see.*

Recommendations for best practices to teach math (Zemelman, Daniels, and Hyde, 1998) to elementary-age children include cooperative group work, the discussion of mathematics, the justification of mathematical thinking, and problem solving. These same recommendations stress content integration and teachers as facilitators of learning. Each recommendation is fulfilled when mathematical learning is embedded into projects. With project work, students have real-world reasons to use the mathematics they are learning.

## Social Studies

Because service projects almost always benefit a person or a group of people, the National Social Studies Standards related to "people, places, and environment" and "individuals, groups, and institutions" can be integrated into many projects. Depending on the project, the standards of "time, continuity, and change;" "production, distribution, and consumption;" and "civic ideals and practices" can be integrated into projects. Just as best-practice experts encourage integrating math with other content areas, these same experts (Zemelman, Daniels, and Hyde, 1998) encourage integrating social studies with other disciplines. Projects are a natural way to integrate teaching and learning of knowledge and skills into the content areas.

**Strategies for Teachers**

*Most states include skills related to working in teams, issues related to social groups, and problems of everyday living in their social studies standards. These standards are easily taught and practiced within the context of service projects.*

In some ways, project work best applies to standards for social studies. It is in social studies that teachers present concepts such as needs vs. wants, interdependence of supply and demand, citizenship, and community. These concepts are directly used in project work. During the canned food drive project, students learned about the needs of those less fortunate and used the concept of supply and demand to gauge the number of food items needed. Other projects present the needs of others to the students, as well. When collecting donations for any cause, students are learning to see a situation from another point of view and realize that their views of the world are not the only ones.

# Science

Perhaps it is more difficult to integrate science skills into service projects than any other content area. However, in the broader sense of science, science skills integrate easily into projects. Students' investigative skills are often used in projects as children ask questions, make observations, organize data, explain their positions or data, reflect on the processes used or roadblocks encountered, and take action. Students also use science throughout project work. That is, they do hands-on activities instead of just watching. Projects often call for the use of technology, using computers not only for word processing, but for analyzing data, charting, or making comparisons.

If time for projects is limited because of standards and objectives, then service projects can be chosen more carefully, presenting to children those projects that specifically address science standards and objectives. Some examples are:

- Planting and caring for different types of plants to beautify the school grounds covers standards and objectives related to earth science.
- Creating landscape photographs to beautify a nursing home covers standards and objectives related to different landforms.
- Organizing an evening astronomy night for the school so that students can observe the night sky relates to standards about astronomy.
- Spearheading a family fitness opportunity (sponsoring a "run," encouraging regular exercise, etc.) covers standards related to life science.
- Making safety inspections of the school. Offering "kits" so that students can inspect their homes relates to responsible energy use.

# Thinking and Reasoning Skills

Service projects also promote development of thinking and reasoning skills. Problems are an integral part of any project. Some problems can be anticipated, while others emerge as the project proceeds. Either way, solving these problems requires higher-level thinking skills. Among the thinking and reasoning skills that projects enhance are:

- identifying multiple resources that relate to a single topic
- evaluating information to determine what is most relevant and reliable
- brainstorming multiple solutions to a problem
- making decisions based on rationale
- analyzing information from multiple resources

## Strategies for Teachers

*Look through the state-mandated skills for grade-level math, science, and social studies. Put an asterisk beside each skill that could be taught within the context of a service project. Also, look at the skills to determine which can be combined or tweaked so that a project can cover multiple standards.*

- synthesizing information
- comparing and contrasting different perspectives

Children learn each skill as they work through projects. Since it is important to students that their projects succeed, solving project-related problems should be important to them. Just as students learn more knowledge and skills within the context of projects, students develop thinking and reasoning skills more deeply when they are involved with something that is important to them.

## Learning How to Learn

In addition to academic content and specific thinking skills, service projects help students learn how to learn. After completing one project, students can apply the same steps to a different project. Projects typically go through the following stages: initial planning, creating committees, determining due dates, holding planning and check-in meetings, tracking, and wrapping up. After students have learned these basic steps, they are more likely to understand what it takes to plan and implement a project, take on decision making and problem solving without prompting, understand how to gather information, and know how to research a topic.

## Summary

As students work on service-learning projects, they can learn important knowledge and skills from the disciplines of reading, writing, math, science, and social studies when these skills are embedded into a project. Students also learn thinking and reasoning skills, and when they work on multiple projects in an academic year, students literally learn how to learn.

# Social and Emotional Development in Service Projects

During elementary school, children grow from relatively dependent young children into fairly independent children entering adolescence. Not only do children begin to set their academic foundations, they also establish who they will be socially and emotionally. Learning these social and emotional nuances is important to elementary-age children. Children are developing skills that help them deal with social situations ranging from behaving in groups to interacting with other individuals. The emotional skills established in these early years can influence how children deal with issues throughout their lives.

Children's social and emotional development includes knowledge of self and others. During the elementary years, children learn to exhibit self-control and accept personal responsibility. They also build relationships of mutual trust and respect with others, and learn to work cooperatively. They learn to adapt to different environments, and express their feelings through appropriate gestures, actions, and language. They develop strong friendships and learn to respect the rights of others as well as similarities and differences among people. They learn to examine situations from other people's perspectives and to resolve conflicts with others.

Some elementary schools focus on experiences that support the social and emotional development of children. However, many do not. No matter which approach a school takes, the very act of being with peers at school requires social interactions and emotional encounters. Being involved in service projects not only enhances children's social and emotional development without making judgments about the "correct" way to teach it, but service learning also fosters personal skills often referred to as "megaskills."

## Enhancing Children's Social-Emotional Development

The social and emotional development of elementary-age children includes developing proficiency in a wide range of areas. When working in service projects, children have opportunities to practice and refine this development. The social and emotional skills enhanced through project work include both interactions with others and individual qualities.

### Interactions with Others

Work on service projects often occurs in small groups. Children have a variety of opportunities to work with groups of peers while learning the skills that make teamwork effective and efficient. While some children may intuitively know how to work in small groups (or figure out some effective strategies on their own), all children benefit when teachers formally present skills related to group work.

No matter the age of the participants, the give-and-take of small group dynamics calls for all participants to be agreeable. Learning to be agreeable is one of the first skills project teachers emphasize. This skill includes respecting other people's property and space, active listening, and seeing others' perspectives. It seems obvious to adults

that group members should not do things like sit too close to someone, use other people's pencils or markers, write on each other's papers, or display other inappropriate behaviors. However, these are not always clear to children. Even students who have been in school for several years benefit from conversations about social behaviors that are appropriate for group work.

Families want their children to be agreeable and they are always searching for ways to instill this quality in their children. A family letter outlining the guidelines the teacher and the children are establishing informs families of class expectations.

As children become aware of the social nature of their interactions, they also practice other social skills. That is, children learn to listen when others are speaking and how to demonstrate this by paraphrasing what others say and by practicing active listening strategies. Children benefit from understanding and appreciating the differences and/or similarities between themselves and others. They develop a sense of open-mindedness while learning the give-and-take of negotiation. They learn to adapt and see value in others' suggestions. They learn that certain situations call for leading, and others for following.

> **Strategies for Teachers**
>
> *Consider the steps involved in a simple task you ask children to do, such as coming to a group area. Think through the task and write down each step. Be very detailed in the list so that nothing is overlooked. Think through the best way to accomplish each step. Then, when you teach that routine to the class, you have analyzed the task and established an efficient plan for accomplishing it.*

These are skills that may develop over time, but children begin demonstrating these prosocial behaviors during group work sooner if teachers explain why these behaviors are important. Teachers should model the behaviors, and lead children through practicing these behaviors during class meetings. Then, as children work together in large and small groups, they become more attuned to helping each other, supporting each other, and working together toward a common goal. They exhibit flexible and adaptable behavior in changing settings. These are behaviors that come with enhanced social and emotional development.

## Individual Qualities

In 1991, the Secretary of Labor asked the Secretary's Commission on Achieving Necessary Skills (SCANS) to determine skills young people need to succeed in the high-performance workplace (U. S. Department of Labor). Their report, "What Work Requires of Schools," outlines foundational skills (the basic skills of reading, writing, mathematics, listening, and speaking); thinking skills (such as creative thinking, decision making, problem solving, imagining, knowing how to learn, and reasoning); and personal qualities (responsibility, self-esteem, sociability, self-management, and integrity/honesty).

While achieving these individual qualities might seem out of reach in elementary school, children can begin learning and honing these skills. Project work supports students learning the SCANS thinking skills and personal qualities as well as others, such as:

* controlling impulses
* showing increasing independence in planning and carrying out activities

- considering the consequences of actions
- taking care of personal needs
- self-esteem
- planning ahead
- developing a questioning frame of mind to encourage hypothesizing, testing, and evaluating data
- asking for what is wanted
- conveying feelings in appropriate, socially acceptable ways

## Fostering Personal Skills

Through working on service-learning projects, children also develop certain personal skills, often referred to as "megaskills" (Rich, 1997). The 11 megaskills are:

- confidence
- motivation
- effort
- responsibility
- initiative
- perseverance
- teamwork
- common sense
- problem solving
- focus
- caring

These megaskills, along with the SCANS thinking skills and personal qualities, address many of the same issues. Elementary-age children can develop these megaskills as they work on service projects.

Confidence is a person's belief in his or her own abilities. It takes confidence to try new things. People develop confidence over time when they successfully complete tasks on their own. This is particularly true for children in elementary school. So, it is important that children undertake tasks that are complex enough to be challenging, yet simple enough for them to accomplish. Service-learning projects offer a context for confidence-building in young children. During the course of projects, students undertake many tasks both individually and in small groups (after some instruction/teaching from adults or more competent students). They may make telephone calls to "experts" to find answers to questions the class has; research the answers to questions from other sources, such as books, magazines, brochures, Web sites, etc.; write letters and receive information from different sources; and present information to various audiences. Completing any of these tasks helps children begin to see themselves as capable of doing important work. Children's confidence grows when they view themselves as capable people.

Defining motivation is more difficult. In a way, motivation is simply wanting to do something. Teachers and parents want children to be internally motivated and eager to learn. They also want children to do school work

and household chores without being nagged, and to make plans for the next day and the next week. However, external motivation is necessary to help children develop internal motivation. When children work on service projects, there is always an external motivation—people who benefit from the project.

Effort is the willingness to work hard. Many elementary-age students want to give up when school work gets too difficult. Service projects support children as they learn the value of effort. The sense of working together and helping those who truly need help gives children an added desire to work hard. As they work through projects, most children realize that they must put forth a certain amount of effort, even when the work gets difficult. Without this effort, the project will never be finished, and the people who might benefit from the project will never be helped.

A sense of responsibility helps children do what is right in relation to their school work, home life, and relationships with friends and family. Learning to accept responsibility for actions is a valuable life-long skill that is fostered by project work.

Initiative is the readiness to move into action. Children learn initiative as they see parts of a project that need completing. At first, most students volunteer for tasks that have been identified by the group, but over time, and with multiple experiences with service projects, students begin doing different parts of a project just because they need to be done. By taking on a task themselves and carrying it to completion, students learn to show initiative and stretch their limits.

Perseverance is the willingness to continue and complete what is started. Getting children to stick with something, even when it gets hard, is not an easy thing to do. Following through and finishing a plan is not easy, even for adults, but it is different in service projects. Because service projects benefit others, elementary-age children are often willing to stay with a project, even when it gets complicated or problematic. They understand that giving up is a decision that affects other people.

Teamwork is becoming an even more important skill than in previous generations. Understanding how to work as a team member is a skill that is common in adult workplaces. Most workplace conflicts relate to how each member of the team does his or her job. When individual team members are not doing their jobs, the team's work and success suffers.

Common sense is good judgment. Children cannot develop this without being in situations where common sense can be applied. Project teachers constantly give decisions back to children. While they guide the class's direction, teachers expect children to have input and make decisions using common sense.

Problem solving can be viewed as a person putting into action what he or she already knows and can do. Many

times during project work, children face problems that have no obvious solutions or have multiple solutions. With help from the teacher, they have opportunities to negotiate solutions and try them out. They also learn to reevaluate solutions that do not work out as planned.

Focus, the ability to concentrate with a goal in mind, means staying with a job until it is completed. By paying attention to the task at hand, children learn to focus and ignore distractions.

Caring means showing concern for others. Because service projects are based on showing concern for people, children learn to care as they work through a project. Many times, young children care but do not have the means to display their caring nature. Projects empower children as they show concern for others.

Socially competent and emotionally stable children do more than behave in socially acceptable ways. They are problem-solvers who look at situations from different points of view until solutions are generated. Experience with projects guides children along the path to establishing these qualities.

### Establishing Good Citizens for the Future

As elementary-age students work on service projects, they develop important interpersonal and intrapersonal skills. Taken as a whole, these are the characteristics that successful adults possess. These are the characteristics that society needs its good citizens to demonstrate. As elementary children work on service projects, they are preparing to become the good citizens of tomorrow.

## Summary

Many facets of children's social and emotional development, as well as personal qualities and skills, are enhanced through service project work. Over time, children feel good about themselves and begin to see themselves as capable people.

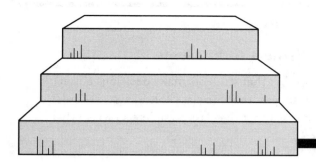

# The Steps in a Service Project

Every service-learning project takes on its own personality. Each project is different because of the focus of the project and the skill level of the students directing the project. As different as projects are, there are certain steps that serve as a framework for project work. Certain things need to be in place before a class begins its first project. Typically, the teacher introduces a project to students, and students consider whether they want to take on this work. Brainstorming starts the initial project planning, then committees of students take responsibility for tasks and set deadlines for their work. The class continues planning meetings for as long as needed, then switches to check-in meetings to ensure that the project is on track. Finally, the project is wrapped up, and students assess their work.

## Before the Project

There is no "right" time to begin a first project with a new group of students. Project teachers believe that a sense of community should be established before beginning project work, so they observe students closely to determine how well that sense of community has been established. It takes a different amount of time for each group of students to begin to view themselves as a "family," but a general guideline is that four to eight weeks are required for a sense of community to develop among a group of students.

When making the decision about when to start a first project, project teachers observe students for certain behaviors related to how children work together. They look for children's ability to make decisions as a group, carry out plans that they agree to, and solve problems with others. Not all students exhibit behaviors necessary for project work at the same time. However, when most students demonstrate these behaviors, teachers can assume that the class is ready to begin their first project.

The physical environment of the classroom also supports project work, so the classroom should be ready for project work. Project teachers provide places for students to meet in small groups while making materials and supplies accessible to all students. Usually a classroom is arranged before the school year begins, but it can always be rearranged to support project work before the class's first project.

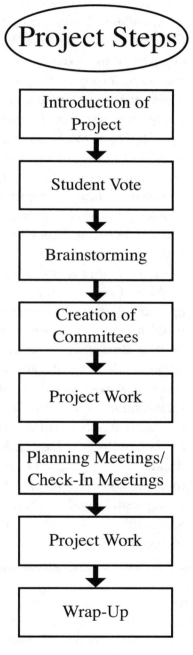

Project Steps

- Introduction of Project
- Student Vote
- Brainstorming
- Creation of Committees
- Project Work
- Planning Meetings/ Check-In Meetings
- Project Work
- Wrap-Up

## Introducing the Project to Students

It is important to remember that students make decisions about projects. Teachers may suggest that the class consider a particular project but should not insist that the class complete a project that students vote against.

When talking with students about a potential project, teachers discuss the need in some detail and explain how doing the project meets that need. More specifically, teachers help children see how their project work affects real people. Even young children are usually interested in working on a project that helps other people, especially other children.

## Initial Planning

Just as the choice of a project is a student decision, the initial planning also comes from the students, usually during a class meeting. The teacher acts as a scribe to record the ideas that children discuss. Typically, initial planning begins with brainstorming a list of tasks that students think might be part of this particular project. It is not important in the first meeting or two that the tasks be listed in any particular order. Getting the ideas in written form is the goal of initial planning.

However, after a couple of meetings, the teacher begins to lead children to think about a system of organizing the tasks. One easy way to do this is to form committees and assign each task on the list to a committee. Sometimes the students take the term "cut and paste" literally and cut apart the tasks previously recorded on chart paper. Then, each committee takes the tasks that relate to their responsibilities. Tasks that are not taken by a committee are often presented to the whole class at a meeting so that children can make decisions about those tasks. At this point, new committees may be formed, current committees may take on more work, or individual children may assume responsibilities for leftover tasks.

## Creating Committees

Project teachers generally discover that children who volunteer for committees work harder and for longer periods of time. Most project teachers encourage children to volunteer for committees. However, most young children tend to volunteer based on social issues. Most of the time, this does not present a problem. But, there are times when a project teacher decides to assign students to committees or asks children to work on certain committees for academic or social reasons. This usually occurs when a child would benefit from working with particular children. If a kindergarten child is struggling to write the sounds he hears in words, he would benefit from working with children who hear letter sounds and connect the appropriate letter with each sound. If two children are experiencing problems with each other, perhaps they should not work on the same committee.

## Creating Due Dates

Elementary school students usually have not had much experience with setting their own deadlines and due dates. Most young children are accustomed to doing school assignments on the day of the assignment. How teachers go about leading students to set deadlines depends on the project itself.

If there is no particular date that a project must be wrapped up, then teachers can be open-ended about deadlines. Leading children to set deadlines might be done with each committee, for example, "How long do you think that it will take this committee to finish the things on their To-Do list?" (page 93). The same approach can be used during a class meeting for setting deadlines that affect the entire class.

If there is a definite date by which a project must be finished, then a teacher might suggest that students work backward from the deadline, for example, "If we only have three weeks to do this project, how many things on your list can you finish by this Friday? Next Friday? The following Friday?"

Whether dates are set by how long students think it will take or working backward from a final date, it will help children stay organized and focused if there is a large calendar posted in the classroom. Students should enter all deadlines on this calendar so that everyone knows when everything is due.

## Holding Planning and Check-In Meetings

In any project, different groups work on different tasks almost every day. Keeping up with who is doing what is important. To make sure everything is on track, project teachers typically hold a meeting to begin each project time. At the beginning of a project, the meetings focus on the planning process. When most of the students are implementing plans, the meetings become check-in meetings.

Planning meetings (Developmental Studies Center, 1996) are frequent at the beginning of a project; however, they can be held at any time during a project if issues arise that require planning.

Planning meetings are typically kept to under 20 minutes (even shorter for kindergarten and first-grade students) because of the attention spans of young children. The teacher almost always acts as a scribe to record the children's ideas. Depending on past experiences related to project work or students' ability to make their own decisions about learning, teachers may need to guide children's thinking during the planning process. Even if it would be faster for project teachers to tell their students what they need to do to accomplish a project, they do not do this. Project teachers make suggestions or ponder, but they do not direct students' decisions. Teachers who effectively use the strategy of pondering lead children without dictating to them (see pages 35-36).

Check-in meetings (Developmental Studies Center, 1996) are usually held on a daily basis during a project. Check-in meetings are usually shorter than planning meetings, often taking only 5-10 minutes. These meetings are held to talk with committees about what they have been doing or to ask if they need extra help to complete their tasks. Sometimes, if one committee is having trouble with a task, the children ask for suggestions from their classmates.

## Tracking Progress

Younger children need a more concrete method of tracking progress than older children do. For kindergarten and first-grade students, long lists of "things to do" work well. Each committee's tasks are listed on a separate To-Do List (see page 93). Then, as one task is completed, a committee member makes a check mark beside the task or draws a line through it.

Older students do not necessarily need large charts to track what they have finished and what they need to do. Teachers may recommend that committee members keep lists in their project folders.

## Wrapping Up the Project

Each project culminates in a final event. Some projects easily lend themselves to this. The canned food drive project had a deadline set by district personnel. The culminating event for this project was boxing the donated food and getting the boxes to the back door of the school to be picked up. Not every project will have such an obvious wrap-up event.

### Note to the Reader

*If students complain that someone on their committee is not doing what she should do, then ask for a meeting with the committee. In the meeting, children should use "I" statements to discuss what they think the problem is. Give examples of "I" statements, such as, "I feel mad when you don't do the things our committee is supposed to do." Ask the child who is being accused if she understands what the other children are saying. Wrap up the meeting by asking students to say what they want from the child and ask the child if she thinks what the group is asking is fair and doable.*

### If . . . Then

*If one committee seems to have trouble staying on track, then meet with that committee at the beginning of each project time and have them outline what they plan to accomplish on that day. Then, check on the committee two or three times during that day's project time to review progress.*

Service Learning Projects for Elementary Students • CD-104032 • © Carson-Dellosa

## If . . . Then

*Sometimes children get stuck while working on projects. At times, the entire class can be stuck, and at other times, just one committee will be stuck. If this occurs, then turn the decision about what to do to the children. A class meeting can gather solutions from the whole group, or, students in committees can brainstorm ways to find the answers to the problem.*

In any case, the end of a project is a time for celebration. While children evaluate their performance throughout the project, their final evaluation of their work is vitally important to learning how to do things better.

## Assessing the Finished Project

Assessing what worked well and identifying problems within a project is a necessary step in project work. Even young children learn more about how to do certain things differently when they are involved in a discussion to evaluate their own work. As in other types of project-related discussions, teachers frequently use the techniques of pondering or wondering aloud (pages 35-36) to guide this discussion. Teachers might use phrases like, "How well do you think the can-counting committee worked? Did everyone on that committee do his job?"

Children also use the evaluation period to write self-assessments. Young children fill in the blanks on open-ended questions or complete checklists that indicate "happy face" and "sad face" behaviors. Older children write short narratives to express their evaluations. Examples of this written self-assessment in reproducible formats can be found on pages 90-91.

It is important to note that, throughout the project, children are constantly assessing their work. Routinely, children determine what the "good" qualities of a piece of work are before they start work on it. Looking at their work within a project is not new to them.

Teachers of young children know that when a task is divided into smaller parts, children find the task easier to complete. The same is true about self-assessments. By assessing the smaller parts of a task, children learn how to look at their work in sections and decide what course would lead to improvements in each section.

There is not a right or wrong time to begin a project, nor is there a "best" first project to use for a class. A project teacher sometimes jumps right in, unsure about a project's success, and things turn out well. Other times, a teacher is deliberate about his decision to begin a project. In either case, a teacher should trust children and respect their ideas, remembering that it is the children's project and the learning that occurs is meaningful, even if it is not the learning he predicted.

## Evaluation of Project

A service project always benefits an audience outside of the class of students who conduct the project. A service project can benefit an individual (perhaps a child who has lost a jacket), a group of people (perhaps children who do not have gloves or mittens in cold weather), or an organization (perhaps a local food bank). As mentioned earlier, young children tend to be egocentric and do not always recognize the needs of those around them, so the teacher usually has to bring the "need" to the attention of the class as they begin service project work. Without guidance from a teacher or another adult, children may have difficulty understanding how they might meet a particular need.

## Summary

While there are many variables within each project, most follow predictable steps. A teacher begins by introducing the project to students. Next, students direct the initial planning phase and create committees to do the tasks. Due dates are created to help the children meet deadlines, and planning and/or check-in meetings keep the project on track. At the end of the project, the children evaluate the project's success and their own involvement, as well.

### If . . . Then

*If students are focused on what classmates did wrong, then redirect their thinking by asking each student to say one thing she thought the class could do better in the next project.*

# Identifying School and Community Needs

A school-based service project can benefit teachers, students, or an entire school community. Likewise, there are needs within the local community that students can support. Both school- and community-based projects can benefit the students and audience, as well.

## School-Based Needs

Within any elementary school, there are many needs that can be met through student-directed service projects. Teachers who are searching for potential service projects should first examine the work that adults in the school do. By reevaluating how their school operates, they often discover that many of the tasks usually done by adults can be done by students, and the children can learn important knowledge and skills in the process. Some elementary schools operate with an informal rule that teachers do not do any work that students can do and learn from themselves.

Included in the Appendix are descriptions of three service projects that respond to needs within schools. The Lost and Found project (page 67) describes one class's way of organizing the school's Lost and Found to more efficiently return lost items to their owners. The PTA Membership Drive project (page 68) outlines how a class assisted the school's PTA in soliciting new members. The Reading Service project (pages 71-72) describes how a group of second-graders created a service to help students who needed help with reading. These service projects are common to many elementary schools, but the work is often done by teachers or other adults in the school community.

On page 58, there are examples of letters that can launch service projects. These projects are straightforward and can be conducted by students at any elementary grade level. However, there are other projects that benefit different school groups. On pages 58-64, there are service projects that can be conducted by elementary-age students. The projects are divided into categories based on who the projects serve: teachers, other students, and/or the whole school community. Each project and its most obvious learning opportunities are described briefly. If only a few learning opportunities are listed under each project, that does not mean that these are the only learning experiences the project provides. Depending on how each project is organized, multiple opportunities exist for further academic learning and affective development. Other service learning projects can be found in the appendix (pages 65-73).

### If . . . Then

*If there does not seem to be a natural way to introduce your service project to a class, consider asking the principal or another teacher in the school to write a memo to the class, asking them to consider accepting the responsibility of a project. See examples on page 58.*

Dear Mrs. Johnson's Class:

This morning, as I was walking to the school from the parking lot, I noticed how dreary the area around our back door looks. There are pebbles from the playground scattered around the area leading to the door. The plants in the container are turning yellow. It just looks kind of sad. I am hoping that you all will take a look at this area and see what you think. Maybe you can work together to come up with a plan to make this part of our school look more inviting. Talk about it and let me know what you think.

Sincerely,

Mrs. Sanchez

*Letter to Students #1*

Dear Mr. Lintz's Class:

My first-grade students want to research reptiles. We started looking for resources in our library yesterday. This morning some students brought in a few books and several pages they had printed from Internet Web sites. The problem is that these resources are written at a level much higher than my students' reading abilities. I was wondering if any of you might be willing to give up a portion of your time to read to my students. Here's my plan. My students would mark passages they want to have read aloud to them, then put the book or other material in a basket near the door. When you came into the class, you could choose something from the basket, call the child's name that is written on the sticky note, then spend about 10 minutes reading to that child. This way you would spend half of your fifth-grade DEAR time in your own class and the other half reading to my first graders. What do you think?

Best regards,
Mrs. Delano

*Letter to Students #2*

# Service Projects That Benefit Teachers

Teachers have multiple responsibilities beyond teaching. Service projects can help relieve teachers of some extra responsibilities while helping students learn different skills.

## Caring for Classrooms Plants

Many teachers think that having plants in the classroom creates a more pleasing environment; however, caring for plants requires time and commitment. By organizing a service project around caring for the plants in the school, students not only help teachers, but they also learn science content. Information about different household plants and what they require in terms of soil, water, light conditions, fertilizer, etc., can all be learned from this project. Students also learn to plan, organize schedules, meet deadlines, and (if they are responsible for purchasing supplies to maintain the plants) budget money wisely.

## Organizing School Supplies

On the first and second days of school, teachers are inundated with school supplies. It takes time to go through each student's bag of supplies, sort like supplies, distribute supplies in the classroom for immediate student use, and store others. Younger children who are adjusting to school are often confused or baffled by what to do with these supplies. Older students can help teachers organize supplies as a short-term service project, which would help students refine organizational skills and learn to set up inventories.

## Organizing Classroom Libraries

It is almost impossible to have too many books in a classroom library, but organizing the books so that students can easily find particular books can be challenging for a teacher. This task is also time consuming. Older elementary students can work with younger students to reorganize classroom libraries, leading decisions as the younger children decide which books should be grouped by author and which should be organized by topic. While working on this project, older students not only refine their organizational and decision-making skills but also learn about leading younger children in making decisions, rather than just telling them what to do.

## Serving as Readers and Facilitators

The time in the morning between when children can come into the classroom and when school formally begins can be a chaotic time in the earlier grades. Older students can organize a service project in which one or two students go to kindergarten or first-grade classrooms to read to or facilitate activities that have been selected by the teacher. Older children's reading skills will be enhanced, but they will also be learning about getting along with younger children.

# Service Projects That Benefit Students

Projects that benefit other students typically involve older students helping younger ones, but this is not always the case. There are several ways that students can work on service projects that benefit all students.

## Serving as a Welcoming Committee

At the beginning of the school year, many students are not familiar with the layout of the school and do not know how to find their assigned classrooms. Students feel "invited" or special when other students are waiting at each school entrance ready to answer questions about this "big, new place" and willing to walk new students to their classrooms. It is important to have welcoming committees during the first week of school, but it is nice to have welcoming committees at each entrance throughout the year. Having someone offer a greeting sets a good tone for the school day. Children who are a part of these welcoming committees learn to communicate with others and learn how to offer a helping hand.

## Offering Conflict Mediation for Other Students

Many elementary schools have conflict resolution programs in which students meet with peers who are having difficulty getting along. The students attend a certain number of training hours to learn how to facilitate conversations between quarreling students and to role-play different scenarios. Most often, adults conduct the training sessions, but students can enlist volunteers for the program, advertise its availability, and schedule conflict mediation sessions. Students working on the organizational parts of this project learn about working with others—about convincing students to volunteer to be conflict mediators and convincing students to use the services of the conflict resolution program.

## Serving as After-School Tutors

Just as students can organize conflict resolution programs to help their peers solve interpersonal problems, they can organize after-school tutoring programs. These programs connect students who need help learning particular concepts or skills with students who feel competent in those concepts or skills.

## Serving as Technology Experts

Teachers know that technology does not always work. Often when there is a problem with a computer, a student has hit a wrong key or accidentally opened an unfamiliar program. With relatively little training, students who are familiar with technology can learn to troubleshoot common problems. This helps students who are having problems and saves teachers' time. This project can be established in a computer lab with technology experts "on duty" at particular times, or in individual classrooms with "experts" trained from each class. These troubleshooters refine their technology skills while teaching those skills to others.

## Serving as Readers

When kindergarten and first-grade students research particular topics, many resources they locate are written at levels beyond their reading abilities. Older students can organize a "Reading Service" in which they visit early childhood classrooms during the class's inquiry time and read portions of expository texts, magazine and newspaper articles, brochures, etc., to younger students. Younger students benefit from this service. Older students enhance their abilities to use reading strategies to read unfamiliar text and learn how to restate what they read by explaining different parts of the text in response to the younger students' questions.

## Teaching Fire Safety

Fire safety is typically taught by teachers. However, this is a topic that students can research. Based on their research, they can create a live presentation for other classes or create a video to show to other classes. In addition to the content learned through research, students also learn about writing scripts or producing informational videos.

## Organizing School Buddies

Many elementary schools foster relationships across grade levels. Some use reading to each other as the basis for "buddy" relationships. Some schools organize social times when pairs of classes get together to sing, participate in movement activities, or share recess time. Students can organize "Buddy Programs" and plan social events that encourage a stronger sense of school community. As a class works on this type of project, students learn about scheduling, working out logistical problems, surveying students to find out what types of social events most students would prefer, planning events, and implementing their plans.

# Service Projects That Benefit the Entire School Community

## "Getting to Know You" Bulletin Board

When a class assumes responsibility for the "Getting to Know You" bulletin board, they interview each faculty and staff member and write a brief biography about each person. Students design a bulletin board to display photographs, biographies, and answers to standard interview questions that give some insight into the teacher/staff members' personalities. Questions might include, "Why did you want to work with children?," "What do you like best about being at school?," "What is your favorite book? Movie? Song?" Students learn many language arts skills as well as design principles through this project.

## Organizing Mentor Families

Often, elementary schools match families who are new to the school with families who have been part of the school for a few years. This puts new families in contact with people they can talk to, ask questions of, and share information with. Elementary students are just as capable of completing this "matching" task as teachers. They learn organizational skills while learning to answer questions and offer support.

## Making Signs for the School

Few elementary schools have sufficient signage to help school visitors find their way around. Each school year, a class can research the signs that are needed and create aesthetically pleasing signs. In addition to standard signs that identify classrooms, labs, offices, and rest rooms, students can think about other signs that would be helpful, for example, signs that let visitors know where students are if they are not in their classrooms (at lunch, in the library, at recess, in P.E., in the art studio, etc.). Students learn to design clear, easy-to-read signs while applying language arts skills.

## Beautifying Part of the School Grounds

Most elementary schools would benefit from beautification projects. Students could take on projects as large as planting flower beds on the school grounds or as small as planting containers and placing the containers near the school entrance. Students could research quotations about learning made by famous people and create signs of these to post throughout the school. In the school library or media center, students could add plants, create book jacket displays, intersperse student-created sculptures among the books, etc. These are just a few things students might do to make the school "look better." The learning in this service project would depend on what beautification project the children completed.

## Organizing Carnivals/Festivals

At most elementary schools, adults plan and organize events like carnivals. Students in elementary school are capable of planning these events. One class can plan the carnival and ask each class to create and staff one booth. The carnival or festival might take on a specific theme, such as Math-tacular where all booths relate to math concepts or skills or an Intercultural Festival where each booth represents a different culture or country. As a class organizes a carnival, they learn about planning events, enlisting the support of other classes, working out logistical problems, and overseeing the plans and progress of other classes.

## Organizing the School's Kindergarten Orientation

Most elementary schools have a program for parents of incoming kindergarten students. Typically, the kindergarten curriculum is described, hints for smoother transitions into school are given, and forms are distributed. Usually faculty and staff organize this event, but children can be in charge of this event.

## Planning Promotion Exercises

Students can also organize the end-of-year promotion exercises. They can consult with people who have organized these events in past years, plan the event, and work with adults in the school family to complete tasks.

> **Note to the Reader**
>
> *Identify at least one other teacher in your school who would be willing to help you think about needs in your school that could be met by student-directed service projects. Brainstorm a list of these needs, then choose one or two. Outline a project that would meet those needs. Select the strongest outline. Set a meeting with the principal and ask for support for starting a service project with your class.*

## Organizing a "Kindness and Justice" Challenge

In honor of Martin Luther King, Jr., a group of educators and sponsors called *Do Something* initiated the "Kindness and Justice" Challenge. (Information about this organization can be found at www.dosomething. org.) Included on the Web site are age-appropriate curricula, tied to National Assessment of Eductional Progress (NAEP) core curriculum content standards. One class can organize this challenge for the school. Classes are asked to document the acts of kindness (helping others) and justice (standing up for what's right) for two weeks following the King holiday in January. The organizing class collects the documentation and creates a way, such as a bulletin board, to share these acts with the entire school. As children research the "Kindness and Justice" Challenge, they refine their technology skills. As they create the bulletin board, they learn about issues of design, for example color, balance, and other factors that constitute a pleasing display. Math skills related to graphing can easily be incorporated into this project.

## Volunteering as Library Assistants

Younger children often need help choosing or checking out library books. A class could organize a group of library assistants, made up of older students who help in the library before or after school or during a period of time in the school day when they can be out of their classrooms. The organizing class could develop a training session to teach volunteers how to use the library's check-out system and how to ask questions to help other students make book selections. Working on the organizational part of this project would help students learn to write persuasive speeches (to use to enlist volunteers), create training sessions, and work out schedules. Volunteering to be library assistants would enhance students' interpersonal skills and increase their knowledge about the school's library and its holdings.

## Organizing School Dismissal

Dismissal time in elementary schools can be chaotic. Some children ride home on school buses. Some are picked up by vans for after-school programs. Many are picked up by parents. Children from all classes try to find the vehicles they need. As a service project, older students could observe the dismissal period during the first week of school, then make recommendations for making dismissal more efficient. They could present their plan to the principal and, with approval, send the plan home to families. Students on this committee could go outside just before dismissal time to help direct traffic and organize groups of children who are waiting for buses, vans, and cars.

## Collecting "Box Tops for Education"

Several corporations offer special programs in which they donate learning materials and/or equipment to schools that show proof that their school families purchase their products. Usually this takes the form of collecting box tops, labels from cans, or specific "proof of purchase" sections of the foods' packaging. A single class could decide to organize this drive for the school. They might create advertising posters; write memos to families; send E-mail reminders; and ask school families for the addresses of grandparents, aunts, uncles, etc., and send letters to these people. Students would develop strategies for collecting the proofs of purchase, keeping running totals of everything they collect, and making decisions about what items they will order for the school.

## Organizing Members for Percentage of Sales to Schools

There are several companies that have special programs to benefit schools. Some programs give a small percentage of sales to qualified buyers to individual schools. Some programs allow schools to buy equipment with box tops, labels, or other proofs of purchase. For any of these programs, students can organize ways to get school families involved. Students can also track donations and help decide how the collected funds will be used.

# Community-Based Needs

There are many needs outside the school that can become the base for service projects for elementary-age children. Every city is different. Each has many organizations that help people in need. Each has cultural organizations that rely on philanthropy. Service projects could be organized so that classes work in collaboration with these organizations.

Some service projects that respond to meeting community needs are described in the Appendix. The Canned Food Drive project (pages 10-18), Mittens and Gloves Tree project (page 66), and Book Drive project (pages 69-70) are all examples of projects that meet community needs.

Each of these projects can be conducted in any elementary school. There are other community-based service projects that can be done in any school. Some of these include:

- holding a clothing drive for less fortunate families
- providing holiday meals for less fortunate families
- making lunches on a regular basis for the homeless
- volunteering on-site for an organization on a regular basis
- selling items to raise money to make a donation to a specific organization

Some service projects are dependent on the types of organizations that exist within the school's community. These service projects might include:

- putting together a team for a run to benefit a local cause
- asking for donations to support medical research

## If . . . Then

*If you are having trouble deciding on one organization to support, then write a letter to the families of students and ask if parents volunteer for a local organization. The relationship that the parent has already established with the organization will help as you try to set up a new collaboration between a class of elementary-age students and the organization.*

## Note to the Reader

*Consider the nonprofit organizations in your community that might consider collaborating with elementary students. Prepare a brief proposal explaining how an organization would benefit from this collaboration. Attach an explanation of what students would learn as they worked on a service project that would benefit the organization. Ask if they would consider a partnership, and what steps would need to be taken to formalize the collaboration.*

- "adopting" a zoo animal
- targeting and enlisting new members of a local museum
- collecting new books to donate to a local library
- raising money to help a family pay for an expensive surgery

## Summary

Teachers who experiment with service projects with their elementary-age students will observe dramatic differences in their students. Students leave service-learning classrooms better team workers, better decision makers, better problem solvers, and much more empathic toward others. And, they are more knowledgeable and academically competent than before they completed service projects. Because of their involvement in service projects, students gain many things, but do not sacrifice academic learning because content is embedded within each project.

# Appendix

## Coupons for All Project

### Overview of Project

This project can be completed across grade levels. Younger children are fascinated with the coupon inserts delivered in the newspaper or found in magazines, while older children are intrigued by the idea of saving money. The simplicity of this project makes it a good first project for nonreaders or for small groups. Children cut out coupons from magazines or other sources, sort them into categories, design a distribution system, and offer them for families' use. One distribution system is to attach small envelopes to a poster board, label the envelopes with categories, and place coupons in the corresponding envelopes. Often the categories need to be broad, such as *Cleaning* for coupons for dish washing liquid, bathtub scrub, floor care products, etc., *Pets* for dog food, flea/tick medication, etc., and *Paper* for paper towels, napkins, toilet paper, etc. Students should post instructions nearby to encourage people to take the coupons they need. Coupons should be reviewed periodically to remove expired coupons and add new ones. The project's end is flexible. It can be phased out when interest wanes or after a designated period of time. Children should advertise the service with posters around the school and with flyers distributed to families.

### General Time Line

Initial planning takes one or two weeks. Children need to create the distribution system, collect and cut out coupons, sort coupons, and post the distribution instructions. Advertisement of the service can be ongoing, with flyers sent home to begin the service and periodically after that. School-wide announcements or presentations to individual classes can be made at any time.

### Committees and Their Responsibilities

- **Organizers**—collect coupon inserts from newspapers (or other sources), designate categories, sort coupons into categories, place coupons in holders, write memos seeking permission as needed, create labels and signage as needed
- **Cutting Committee**—monitor for safe scissor use as students cut out coupons
- **Expiration Date**—remove expired coupons from display
- **Advertising**—prepare and distribute flyers for families, write script for and make announcements, plan and present oral presentations to classes, create and display posters

### Possible Work Products

- memo to principal requesting permission to conduct project
- scripts for morning announcements
- guidelines for "cutting" (designating safe ways to use scissors)
- calendar to mark expiration dates
- advertising flyers
- labels for categories
- signage for display

# Mittens and Gloves Tree Project

## Overview of Project

A Mittens and Gloves Tree project is typically introduced to a school by one class who sponsors the project, and is only completed by schools located in areas where winters are cold and children need mittens or gloves for warmth. A real or paper evergreen tree is set up in a prominent place in the school and decorated with donated mittens and gloves rather than ornaments.

The class that organizes this project advertises the collection of mittens and gloves. The class communicates the community need and specifies who will receive the donations by naming the community organization that will distribute the mittens and gloves to needy families.

## General Time Line

Initial planning and organizational work takes a few days, and the drive typically lasts two to four weeks. One set of advertising posters and flyers can be produced in a few days and used throughout the project. Announcements are made on the school's public announcement system two or three days per week. Students may decide to make the appeals more personal by speaking to each class in the school or by talking with parents who drop off or pick up their children.

## Committees and Their Responsibilities

- **Advertising**—make posters and/or flyers informing students, faculty, staff, and families about the need and what to do if they want to donate mittens or gloves
- **Announcements**—draft scripts for announcements, ask classmates to help revise announcements, practice reading the script fluently and with expression, get permission to make the announcements, read announcements over the public-address system
- **Solicitors**—talk with individuals or classes to ask for donations
- **Shoppers**—identify stores that sell gloves and mittens, price items, create a brochure or flyer to distribute to families in the school and other potential donors
- **Gift Receivers**— be near the tree at certain times of the day, usually before and after school, to help those donating gloves and mittens put them on the tree
- **Treasurers**—maintain a running total of gifts: child-size mittens, child-size gloves, adult-size mittens, adult-size gloves

## Possible Work Products
- memo to principal requesting permission to conduct project
- letters to the community organization that will receive the mittens and gloves
- scripts for announcements
- informational signs and flyers

# School Lost and Found Project

## Overview of Project

Being responsible for the needs of the school's Lost and Found is a good first project for elementary-age students. Introduce it to children early in the school year. Typically, many items are lost by the sixth week of school and are stored in the school office. There is usually not a system for connecting a lost item to its owner. A class that assumes responsibility for the Lost and Found organizes the lost items and tries to find each item's owner through flyers, announcements, and "fashion shows." (Students parade through classrooms once a week wearing or carrying lost items.) At the end of the year or semester, items not claimed are donated to a local charity.

## General Time Line

Initial planning and organizational work takes two to three weeks. Announcements are made once or twice a week. Flyers are sent home once every two weeks. "Fashion shows" are scheduled once every week or two, depending on the number of lost items. Informational posters are changed at least once a month.

## Committees and Their Responsibilities

- **Organizers**—sort lost items and arrange them so that children looking for lost items can easily scan items in the Lost and Found
- **Announcements**—draft scripts for morning announcements, ask classmates to help revise announcements, practice reading the script fluently and with expression, get permission to make announcements, read announcements over the public-address system
- **Detectives**—search playground at the end of recess for coats, sweaters, and toys; search cafeteria at the end of lunch for lunch boxes and other items
- **Fashion Show**—organize which student will wear or carry each item, tell all teachers what time the fashion show will be in each room
- **Advertising**—construct signs informing students, faculty, and staff where Lost and Found items are stored, create flyers informing school and families about specific items that have been found
- **Donations**—research places where lost items can be donated

## Possible Work Products

- memo to principal requesting permission to conduct project
- memo to principal requesting permission to make announcements
- scripts for announcements
- memo to teachers about fashion show
- informational signs and flyers
- graph of amount of lost items by type

# PTA Membership Drive Project

## Overview of Project

In most elementary schools, former members of the Parent-Teacher Association (PTA) solicit members for the new school year. However, elementary-age students are capable of running this type of membership drive. The drive involves advertising, asking parents and other family members to join, acknowledging new members, keeping track of who has joined, and maintaining a database of members. It also involves collecting dues and balancing the money collected.

## General Time Line

Drafting letters and flyers and setting up the logistics of soliciting, acknowledging, and tracking new members takes about one week. Soliciting, acknowledging, and tracking new members continues until the membership drive is concluded. The drive typically lasts four to six weeks.

## Committees and Their Responsibilities

- **Grade Level Representatives**—give membership request letter to students, make presentations to individual classes to encourage students to get their family members to become PTA members
- **Membership Letter**—write a letter to send home to families, make copies, distribute letter to students
- **Data Input**—type member names, addresses, telephone numbers, and other data into a database
- **Tellers**—tally money collected as dues each day, record information on individual class lists, keep running total of amount collected, balance totals
- **Thank-You Letter**—write a letter acknowledging membership, ensure that every new member receives a letter
- **Membership Card**—distribute membership cards to members using previously collected data

## Possible Work Products

- memo to principal requesting permission to conduct project
- letter asking parents and other family members to join PTA
- memo to principal requesting permission to make announcements
- memo to teachers
- scripts for announcements
- informational signs and flyers
- acknowledgment letters to new members
- database of members
- form for recording money collected
- receipts for money collected

# Book Drive Project

## Overview of Project

Almost any grade level will feel successful when organizing a book drive, since there is a tangible result (books are collected). The reasons for beginning this service project can vary: to furnish books to a homeless shelter, to provide reading materials for a free clinic, to help with the literacy of disadvantaged children in an after-school program, etc. No matter what reason the children have for beginning this project, the organization and results are about the same. The class that assumes this responsibility advertises the need for books, oversees book collection, and distributes books to the designated organization. The final distribution can be completed by a small group of students, but it is preferable if all class members can be present for the distribution. Continuing partnerships between children and the organization are likely outcomes. After children and families see and understand the need, they are more likely to continue giving to that organization.

## General Time Line

The planning for this project usually takes about two weeks. The children need time to designate committees, volunteer for committees, create advertisements, and organize the collection system. After the announcements have begun and advertising posters are displayed, the book collection begins. The donations are usually taken for two to three weeks. The project ends with the delivery of books to the organization.

## Committees and Their Responsibilities

- **Advertising posters**—create advertising posters, decide where posters should be placed, seek permission to display posters, remove posters when project is complete, update posters with changes as needed
- **Announcements**—draft scripts for announcements, seek revision and editing assistance for announcements, practice reading the script fluently and with expression, get permission to make announcements, read announcements over the public-address system
- **Classroom Announcements**—schedule announcements with individual classes, coordinate time schedule for announcements, write script, practice oral presentations, give final presentation to classes, follow up by answering questions classes may have
- **Collection**—develop system to count books that are collected (by individual classrooms and whole school as well), maintain records of collections, update graphic representations of collections, physically collect books, devise storage system
- **Donations**—identify possible donors, write solicitation letters to possible donors, arrange for pickup or delivery, follow up with phone calls as needed, write thank-you letters, provide necessary tax donation forms to donors
- **Delivery**—determine way to deliver books to organization, solicit necessary help (possibly from families to deliver books in private cars)
- **Field Trip**—seek permission for trip as required, complete paperwork with office staff, check permission slips from classmates as necessary, coordinate trip with organization, arrange for differences in schedule (Lunch may have to be rearranged, or other classes or teachers may need notification, etc.)
- **Organization Contacts**—coordinate phone calls and written communication with organization, establish contact people, plan notes before phone calls, record results of phone calls, report results to class

## Book Drive Project (continued)

## Possible Work Products

- scripts for school-wide announcements
- memo to principal requesting permission to conduct the project
- memo to principal requesting permission to make announcements
- memo to principal summarizing project results
- memo to organization to organize delivery
- memo to classrooms asking about making announcements
- memo to principal requesting permission to make announcements
- planning notes for phone calls to organization
- notes about results of phone calls
- letters to local bookstores to solicit donations of overruns or extra books
- thank-you letters for donations (to bookstores as well as to individual classrooms)
- advertising posters and informational flyers
- scripts and oral presentations for each classroom
- graphic representation of number of books collected (This can be charted by individual classrooms and by the entire school, as well.)

# Reading Service Project

## Overview of Project

Establishing a Reading Service serves two purposes. It offers an opportunity for children to help other children while practicing reading for an authentic purpose. This project works well with first-grade children and older. Using Public Broadcasting's show Reading Rainbow® as a model, children make recordings of books and present them to children at lower reading levels. The Reading Service can take different directions but usually involves videotaping the children while they read books. The video can also include a review of the book, suggestions for other books by the same author or on the same subject, illustrations, or other information. The videos can be shared with children in lower grades, community organizations such as child care facilities, doctors' offices, etc., anywhere children have a few minutes to watch. Sometimes accompanying class (or individual) activities are created, or children may decide to make audiotapes of the books.

## General Time Line

The initial planning can take one or two weeks. The majority of time is spent as children decide which books to read and practice them. It takes a week or so to create illustrations of the books, as well. Children watch a Reading Rainbow® video to determine the qualities they want to emulate. As a group, they develop guidelines and create a rubric against which to judge their work. The videotaping and evaluation of tapes can take about a week as children watch the videos they have created and redo them as necessary. Creating activities to accompany the videos can take one to two weeks. The establishment of the Reading Service library can take about another week. At the end of the project, children spend several more class sessions evaluating their work.

## Committees and Their Responsibilities

- **Librarians**—establish video lending library, make catalog of possible videos, create check-out system, maintain library
- **Videographers**—prepare equipment (video camera, tripod, blank tapes, etc.), operate the video camera, set up the stage, make copies as needed
- **Advertising**—make posters, flyers, etc., as needed
- **Activity**—create classroom (or individual) activities to accompany the videos

## Possible Work Products

- memo to principal requesting permission to conduct the project
- memo to teachers to establish the need
- memo to principal  requesting permission to make announcements
- memo to teachers seeking permission to survey the classes
- script for oral presentations to determine classes' favorite books
- recommended book list for various grade levels
- surveys of children to determine favorite books
- book reviews
- learning activities to complement each book

## Reading Service Project (continued)

- advertising posters and flyers
- letters to community organizations seeking permission to donate completed videos
- scripts for telephone contacts to community organizations
- scripts for oral presentations to classrooms telling how to use the video library
- instructions detailing how to use the VCR or other technology such as a DVD player
- guidelines for checking videos/books out from the library

# Other Ideas for K-5 Service Projects

- school beautification
- Kindergarten orientation
- cash donations to organizations
- book donations to school library/public library
- zoo animal "adoption"
- sponsorship of charity "runs"
- "readers" and "facilitators"
- conflict resolution mediation
- soup label or box top collections
- creating a butterfly garden
- suggesting solutions for parking lot problems
- making place mats for free-meal delivery programs that assist the sick and elderly
- book and toy collections for less fortunate
- sponsorships for school-wide events, such as an alumni reunion, carnivals, conferences, family education nights, or family social events

# References

Brotherton, P. (2002). *Connecting the Classroom and the Community.* Black Issues in Higher Education, 19(5), 20-25.

Clark, C. T. (2002). Unfolding Narratives of Service Learning: Reflections on Teaching, Literacy, and Positioning in Service Relationships. *Journal of Adolescent and Adult Literacy,* 46(4), 288-298.

dePaola, Tomie. (1989) *The Art Lesson.* New York: Putnam Publishing Group.

Developmental Studies Center. (1996). *Ways We Want Our Class to Be: Class Meetings That Build Commitment to Kindness and Learning.* Oakland, CA: Author.

Diffily, D. and Sassman, C. (2002). *Project-Based Learning with Young Children.* Portsmouth, NH: Heinemann.

Gardner, H. (1993). *Frames of Mind: The Theory of Multiple Intelligences.* New York: Basic Books.

Gehring, J. (2002). Partnerships and Service. *Education Week,* 21(21), 14-15.

Hatch, T. (1990). Social Intelligence in Young Children. Paper delivered at the annual meeting of the American Psychological Association.

Jennings, M. (2001). Two Very Special Service-Learning Projects. *Phi Delta Kappan,* 82 (6), 474-76.

Johnson, K. (2001). Integrating an Affective Component in the Curriculum for Gifted and Talented Students. *Gifted Child Today Magazine,* 24(4), 14-19.

Nelsen, J. (1996). *Positive Discipline.* New York: Random House.

Rich, D. (1997). *MegaSkills: Building Children's Achievement for the Information Age.* Boston: Houghton Mifflin.

Waldstein, F. A. and Reiher, T. C. (2001). Service-Learning and Students' Personal and Civic Development. *Journal of Experiential Education,* 24(1), 7-14.

U. S. Department of Labor. (1991). *What Work Requires of Schools: A SCANS Report for America.* Washington, DC: U. S. Government Printing Office.

Zemelman, S., Daniels, H. and Hyde, A. (1998) *Best Practice: New Standards for Teaching and Learning in America's Schools.* Portsmouth, NH: Heinemann.

# Ideas for Service Projects

| Doing Personal Service Projects | Responding to Needs within the School |
|---|---|
|  |  |
| **Responding to Local Needs** | **Supporting Local Organizations** |
|  |  |

# Phone Call Planning Sheet

| | |
|---|---|
| **Date of Phone Call:** | |
| **Student's Name:** | |
| **Call to:** | |
| **Phone Number:** | |

**Question #1:**

**Question #1 Answer:**

**Question #2:**

**Question #2 Answer:**

**Question #3:**

**Question #3 Answer:**

Service Learning Projects for Elementary Students • CD-104032 • © Carson-Dellosa

# Form for Writing Announcements

**Name:** _____ **Date:** _____

## Announcement

**Who?** _____

_____

**What?** _____

_____

**When?** _____

_____

**Where?** _____

_____

**Why?** _____

_____

# Advertising Planning Sheet

**Type of Advertising:** _____

**Who?** _____

_____

**What?** _____

_____

**When?** _____

_____

**Where?** _____

_____

**Why?** _____

_____

**How?** _____

_____

# Committee Task Sheet

| Date Due | Responsibility | Person in Charge |
|----------|----------------|------------------|
|          |                |                  |
|          |                |                  |
|          |                |                  |
|          |                |                  |
|          |                |                  |
|          |                |                  |
|          |                |                  |
|          |                |                  |
|          |                |                  |
|          |                |                  |
|          |                |                  |
|          |                |                  |

# Bar Graph

**Name:** _____

**Project:** _____  **Date:** _____

| K | 1 | 2 | 3 | 4 | 5 |
|---|---|---|---|---|---|
| 200 | 200 | 200 | 200 | 200 | 200 |
| 190 | 190 | 190 | 190 | 190 | 190 |
| 180 | 180 | 180 | 180 | 180 | 180 |
| 170 | 170 | 170 | 170 | 170 | 170 |
| 160 | 160 | 160 | 160 | 160 | 160 |
| 150 | 150 | 150 | 150 | 150 | 150 |
| 140 | 140 | 140 | 140 | 140 | 140 |
| 130 | 130 | 130 | 130 | 130 | 130 |
| 120 | 120 | 120 | 120 | 120 | 120 |
| 110 | 110 | 110 | 110 | 110 | 110 |
| 100 | 100 | 100 | 100 | 100 | 100 |
| 90 | 90 | 90 | 90 | 90 | 90 |
| 80 | 80 | 80 | 80 | 80 | 80 |
| 70 | 70 | 70 | 70 | 70 | 70 |
| 60 | 60 | 60 | 60 | 60 | 60 |
| 50 | 50 | 50 | 50 | 50 | 50 |
| 40 | 40 | 40 | 40 | 40 | 40 |
| 30 | 30 | 30 | 30 | 30 | 30 |
| 20 | 20 | 20 | 20 | 20 | 20 |
| 10 | 10 | 10 | 10 | 10 | 10 |
| **K** | **1** | **2** | **3** | **4** | **5** |

Service Learning Projects for Elementary Students • CD-104032 • © Carson-Dellosa

# Thermometer Graph

**Name:** _____

**Date:** _____

**Title:** _____

**Goal:** _____

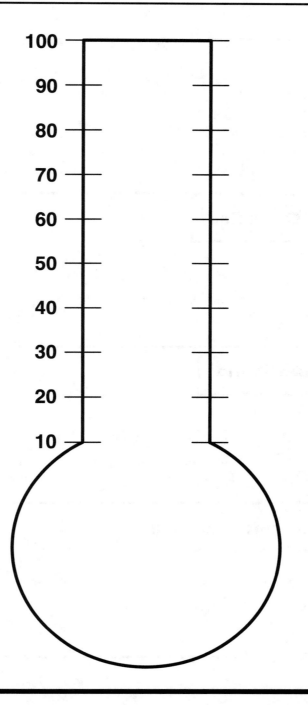

Service Learning Projects for Elementary Students • CD-104032 • © Carson-Dellosa

# Characteristics of Projects

**Student Directed**

**Research Based**

**Multiple Resources Consulted**

**Connected to the Real World**

**Embedded with Knowledge and Skills**

Service Learning Projects for Elementary Students • CD-104032 • © Carson-Dellosa

# Academic Learning Checklist

**Reading** _____

_____

_____

_____

**Writing** _____

_____

_____

_____

**Math** _____

_____

_____

**Social Studies** _____

_____

_____

_____

**Thinking and Reasoning Skills** _____

_____

_____

_____

**Learning How to Learn** _____

_____

_____

_____

Service Learning Projects for Elementary Students • CD-104032 • © Carson-Dellosa

# Supplies List

| Supplies Needed | Supplies Needed |
|---|---|
| _____ | _____ |
| _____ | _____ |
| _____ | _____ |
| _____ | _____ |
| _____ | _____ |
| _____ | _____ |
| _____ | _____ |
| _____ | _____ |
| _____ | _____ |

# Request for Resources Form

Date: _____

Committee Making Request: _____

_____

Topic of Request: _____

_____

Specific Information Needed: _____

_____

_____

Date: _____

Committee Making Request: _____

_____

Topic of Request: _____

_____

Specific Information Needed: _____

_____

_____

# Personal Poem

_____
(first name)

_____
(three adjectives that describe you)

**Lover of...** _____
(three people, things, or ideas)

_____

**Who feels...** _____
(up to three feelings)

_____

**Who needs...** _____
(up to three things)

_____

**Who fears...** _____
(up to three things)

_____

**Who would like to...** _____
(up to three things)

_____

**Am a resident of...** _____
(city, state or province, country)

_____

_____
(last name)

# Personal Interest Bingo

| B | I | N | G | O |
|---|---|---|---|---|
|   |   |   |   |   |
|   |   |   |   |   |
|   |   |   |   |   |
|   |   |   |   |   |
|   |   |   |   |   |

# Thanks Cards

**Thanks to** _____

**for** _____

**Signed** _____

**Thanks to** _____

**for** _____

**Signed** _____

**Thanks to** _____

**for** _____

**Signed** _____

# Respectful Classroom Language

| Instead of... | Think of Saying... |
|---|---|
| Hand me that. | _____ |
| You bumped into me. | _____ |
| You tripped me. | _____ |
| Quit it. | _____ |
| You NEVER pick me! | _____ |
| Shut up. | _____ |
| I'm first. | _____ |
| Leave me alone! | _____ |
| I don't want to! | _____ |
| You took my pencil. | _____ |
| Get your stuff off my desk. | _____ |
| _____ | _____ |
| _____ | _____ |

*Service Learning Projects for Elementary Students* • CD-104032 • © Carson-Dellosa

# Self-Assessment I

**Name:** _____

**Date:** _____

**Name of Project:** _____

| 😊 | ☹️ | I worked with my committee to do the job. |
| 😊 | ☹️ | I was ready to work quickly. |
| 😊 | ☹️ | I stayed on my job and didn't play. |
| 😊 | ☹️ | I cooperated with others. |

**Next time I need to work on** _____

_____

_____

_____

_____

Service Learning Projects for Elementary Students • CD-104032 • © Carson-Dellosa

# Self-Assessment II

**Name:** _____

**Date:** _____

**Name of Project:** _____

_____

**The best thing I did in this project was to:** _____

_____

_____

_____

_____

**Next time I need to:** _____

_____

_____

_____

_____

# Blank Calendar

**Month:** _____

| Sunday | Monday | Tuesday | Wednesday | Thursday | Friday | Saturday |
|--------|--------|---------|-----------|----------|--------|----------|
| | | | | | | |
| | | | | | | |
| | | | | | | |
| | | | | | | |
| | | | | | | |

# To-Do List

| Things To Do | Things To Do |
|---|---|
| _____ | _____ |
| _____ | _____ |
| _____ | _____ |
| _____ | _____ |
| _____ | _____ |
| _____ | _____ |
| _____ | _____ |
| _____ | _____ |
| _____ | _____ |

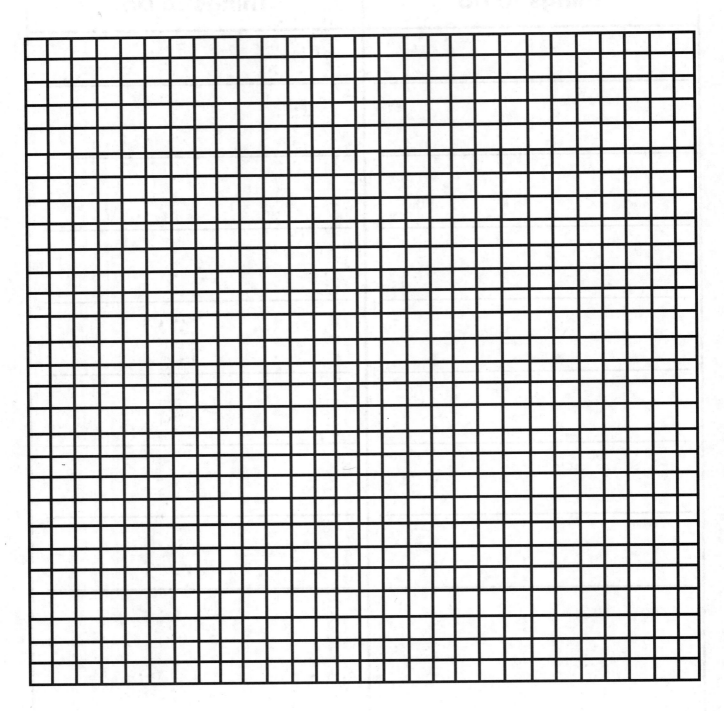

# Voting Chart

**Issue or Question:**

_____

_____

| Yes or Agree | No or Disagree |
|---|---|
| | |

Service Learning Projects for Elementary Students • CD-104032 • © Carson-Dellosa

# Notes